The Anglican Settlement and the Scottish Reformation

The Anglican Settlement and the Scottish Reformation

F. W. Maitland

WIPF & STOCK · Eugene, Oregon

Wipf and Stock Publishers
199 W 8th Ave, Suite 3
Eugene, OR 97401

The Anglican Settlement and the Scottish Reformation
By Maitland, F. W.
ISBN 13: 978-1-5326-1612-9
Publication date 2/1/2017
Previously published by Cambridge University Press, 1934

THE ANGLICAN SETTLEMENT AND THE SCOTTISH REFORMATION.

WHEN at the beginning of 1560 there was a new Pope, pledged to convoke the Council for a third time and to stem and repel the tide of heresy, the latest disaster that met his eye was no mere relapse of England followed by a lapse of Scotland; for what was shaping itself in the northern seas already looked ominously like a Protestant Great Britain. Two small Catholic Powers traditionally at war with each other, the one a satellite of the Habsburg luminary, the other a satellite of France, seemed to be fusing themselves in one Power that might be very great: great perhaps for good, but more probably for evil. "Earnest embracing of religion," wrote a Scottish to an English statesman, "will join us straitly together." The religion that William Maitland meant when he sent these words to Sir William Cecil was not the religion of Pius IV and the General Council.

Suddenly all farsighted eyes had turned to a backward country. Eyes at Rome and eyes at Geneva were fixed on Scotland, and, the further they could peer into the future, the more eager must have been their gaze. And still we look intently at that wonderful scene, the Scotland of Mary Stewart and John Knox: not merely because it is such glorious tragedy, but also because it is such modern history. The fate of the Protestant Reformation was being decided, and the creed of unborn millions in undiscovered lands was being determined. This we see—all too plainly perhaps—if we read the books that year by year men still are writing of Queen Mary and her surroundings. The patient analysis of those love letters in the casket may yet be perturbed by thoughts about religion. Nor is the religious the only interest. A new nation, a British nation, was in the making.

We offer no excuse for having as yet said little of Scotland. Called upon to play for some years a foremost part in the great drama, her entry upon the stage of modern history is late and sudden. In such phrases there must indeed be some untruth, for history is not drama. The annals of Scotland may be so written that the story will be

1

continuous enough. We may see the explosion of 1559 as the effect of causes that had long been at work. We might chronicle the remote beginnings of heresy and the first glimmers of the New Learning. All those signs of the times that we have seen elsewhere in capital letters we might see here in minuscule. Also, it would not escape us that, though in the days of Luther and Calvin resistance to the English and their obstinately impolitic claim of suzerainty still seemed the vital thread of Scottish national existence, inherited enmity was being enfeebled, partly by the multiplying perfidies of venal nobles and the increasing wealth of their paymasters, and partly also by the accumulating proofs that in the new age a Scotland which lived only to help France and hamper England would herself be a poor little Power among the nations: doomed, not only to occasional Floddens and Pinkies, but to continuous misery, anarchy, and obscurity.

All this deserves, and finds, full treatment at the hands of the historians of Scotland. They will also sufficiently warn us that the events of 1560 leave a great deal unchanged. Faith may be changed; works are much what they were, especially the works of the magnates. The blood-feud is no less a blood-feud because one family calls itself Catholic and another calls itself Protestant. The "band" is no less a "band" because it is styled a "Covenant" and makes free with holy names. A King shall be kidnapped, and a King shall be murdered, as of old:—it is the custom of the country. What is new is that farsighted men all Europe over, not only at London and at Paris, but at Rome and at Geneva, should take interest in these barbarous deeds, this customary turmoil.

Continuity there had been and to spare. In that mournful procession of the five Jameses there is no break (1406–1542). The last of them is engaged in the old task, and failing as his forbears failed. It is picturesque; sometimes it is heroic; often it is pathetic; but it is never modern. Modern history sees it as a funeral procession burying a dead time, and we are silent while it passes. In a few sentences we make our way towards the momentous years.

Scotland had been slow to emerge from the Middle Age. A country which of all others demanded strong and steady government had been plagued by a series of infant Kings and contested Regencies. In the sixteenth century its barons still belonged to the twelfth, despite a thin veneer of French manners. Its institutions were rudimentary; its Parliaments were feudal assemblies. Since the close of the War of Independence there had been hardly anything that could properly be called constitutional growth. Sometimes there was a little imitation of England and sometimes a little imitation of France, the King appearing as a more or less radical reformer. But the King died young, leaving an infant son, and his feudatories had no desire for reformation. The

Scottish monarchy, if monarchy it may be called, was indeed strictly limited; but the limits were set much rather by the power of certain noble families and their numerous retainers than by an assembly of Estates expressing the constant will of an organised community. The prelates, lords, and represented boroughs formed but one Chamber. Attempts to induce the lesser tenants-in-chief to choose representatives who would resemble the English knights of the shire had been abortive, and a bad habit prevailed of delegating the work of a Parliament to a committee known as "the Lords of the Articles." Normally the assembly of Estates was but the registrar of foregone conclusions. In troublous times (and the times were often troublous) the faction that was in power would hold a Parliament, and the other faction would prudently abstain from attendance. When in 1560 an unusually full, free and important Parliament was held for the reformation of religion, an elementary question concerning the right of the minor barons to sit and vote was still debateable, and for many years afterwards those who desire to see the true contribution of Scotland to the history of representative institutions will look, not to the blighted and stunted conclave of the three Estates with its titular Bishops and Abbots commendatory, but to the fresh and vigorous Assembly of the Presbyterian Church.

Steady taxation and all that it implies had been out of the question. The Scots were ready to fight for their King, unless they happened to be fighting against him; but they would not provide him with a revenue adequate for the maintenance of public order. He was expected "to live of his own" in medieval fashion, and his own was not enough to raise him high above his barons. Moreover, Douglases and Hamiltons and others, hereditary sheriffs and possessors of "regalities," were slow to forget that these crowned stewards of Scotland were no better than themselves. What had "come with a lass" might "go with a lass," and was in no wise mysterious. We shall see Queen Mary, widow of a King of France, giving her hand first to a Lennox-Stewart whose mother is a Douglas and then to a Hepburn, while the heir presumptive to the throne is the head of the Hamiltons. We shall see Queen Elizabeth having trouble with northern earls, with Percies and Nevilles, who set up an altar which she had cast down, and belike would have cast down an altar which she had set up; but their power to disturb England was as nothing to the power of disturbing Scotland which was exercised by those near neighbours and like-minded fellows of theirs who joined the bellicose Congregation of Jesus Christ. And even in the briefest sketch we must not omit to notice that, as beyond England lay Scotland, so beyond the historic Scotland lay the unhistoric land of "the savages." The very means that had been taken by Scottish Kings to make Scotsmen of these "red-shanks" and to bring these savages within the pale of history had raised up new feudatories of almost royal rank and of more than baronial turbulence. Thenceforward, the King would have to reckon, not only with an Albany, an Angus, and an Arran, but also with an Argyll and with a Huntly. When we see these things we think of the dark age: of Charles the Simple and Rolf the Pirate.

Neither valorous feats of arms which overtaxed a people's strength nor a superabundance of earls and barons should conceal from us the nakedness of the land. It is more than probable that in the middle of the sixteenth century the whole of the Scottish nation, including untamable Highlanders, was not too large to be commodiously housed in the Glasgow of to-day. Life was short, and death was violent. It is true that many hopeful signs of increasing prosperity and enlightenment are visible in the days of James IV (1488–1513). But those days ended at Flodden. The flowers of the forest were once more mown down. The hand went back upon the dial towards poverty and barbarity. An aptitude for letters we may see. Of a brief springtime of song Scotland may fairly boast, for as yet no icy wind was blowing from Geneva. Universities we may see: more universities indeed than the country could well support. By a memorable, if futile, Act of Parliament James IV attempted to drive the sons of the gentry into the grammar-schools. But an all-pervading lack of wealth and of the habits that make for wealth was an impediment to every good endeavour. The printing press had been in no hurry to reach England (1477); but thirty years more elapsed before it entered Scotland. An aptitude for jurisprudence we might infer from subsequent history; but it is matter of inference. Of lawyers who were not ecclesiastics, of temporal lawyers comparable to the professionally learned justices and serjeants of England, we can hardly read a word. When at length James V founded the College of Justice (1532), half the seats in it, and indeed one more, were allotted to the clergy, and in later days foreign science was imported from the continental universities to supply the deficiencies of an undeveloped system. Scotland had been no place for lawyers, and the temporal law that might be had there, though it came of an excellent stock, had for the more part been of the bookless kind. And as with jurisprudence, so with statesmanship. The Scottish statesman who was not a Bishop was a man of a new kind when Lethington began his correspondence with Cecil; for, even if we employ a medieval standard, we can hardly attribute statecraft or policy to the Albanys and Anguses and Arrans.

In this poor and sparsely peopled country the Church was wealthy; the clergy were numerous, laic, and lazy. The names of "dumb dogs" and "idle bellies" which the new preachers fixed upon them had not been unearned. Nowhere else was there a seed-plot better prepared for revolutionary ideas of a religious sort. Nowhere else would an intelligible Bible be a newer book, or a sermon kindle stranger fires. Nowhere else would the pious champions of the Catholic faith be compelled to say so much that was evil of those who should have been their pastors. Abuses which had been superficial and sporadic in England were widely spread and deeply rooted in the northern kingdom. In particular, the commendation of ecclesiastical benefices to laymen, to babies, had become a matter of course. The Lord James Stewart, the King's base-born son, who at the critical moment is Prior of St Andrews and sits in Parliament as a member of the spiritual Estate, is a typical figure. The corslet had "clattered" beneath the Archbishop's cassock, and when Bishops and Abbots lie among the dead on Flodden field they have done no less but no more than their duty. We say that the Scottish Church was rich, and so it nominally was, for the kirk-lands were broad; but when the Protestant ministers, much to their own disappointment, had to be content with a very small fraction of the old ecclesiastical revenues, they had probably secured a larger share than had for a long time past been devoted to any purpose more spiritual than the sustentation of royal, episcopal, and baronial families. We exclaim against the greedy nobles whose lust for the kirk-lands is one of the operative forces in the history of the Scottish Reformation. They might have said that they were only rearranging on a reasonable and modern basis what had long been for practical purposes the property of their class. Their doings send back our thoughts to far-off Carolingian days, when the "benefice" became the hereditary fief. To the King it was, no doubt, convenient that the power of those nobles who would leave heirs should be balanced by the power of other nobles, called prelates, whose children would not be legitimate. But such a system could not be stable, and might at any time provoke an overwhelming outcry for its destruction, if ever one bold man raised his voice against it. Men who are not themselves very moral can feel genuine indignation when they detect immorality among those who, though no worse than themselves, pretend to superior holiness. Prelates, and even primates of Scotland, who were bastards and the begetters of bastards, were the principal fore-runners and coadjutors of John Knox; and unfortunately they were debarred by professional rules from pleading that they, or the best among them, were in truth the respectable husbands of virtuous wives.

Lollardy too there had been, and in some corners of the land it had never been thoroughly extirpated. Also there had been a little burning, but far from enough to accustom the Scots to the sight of a heretic tortured by the flames. Then the German leaven began to work, and from 1528 onwards a few Lutherans were burnt. The protomartyr was Patrick Hamilton, the young and well born Abbot of Ferne. Like many another Scottish youth he had been at the University of Paris. Afterwards he had made a pilgrimage, if not to Wittenberg, at all events to Marburg. It is characteristic of time and place that historians have to consider whether a feud between Douglases and Hamiltons counts for nothing in his martyrdom. "The reek of Patrick Hamilton," we are told, infected many; and we can well believe it. The College of St Leonard was tainted with humanism and new theology. Young men fled from Scotland and made fame elsewhere. Such were Alexander Aless, who as Alesius became the friend of Melanchthon, and John Macalpine, who as Machabaeus professed divinity at Copenhagen. Such also was George Buchanan, the humanist and the Calvinist, the tutor and the calumniator of Queen Mary. And we see the Wedderburns who are teaching Scotsmen to sing ballads of a novel kind, "good and godly ballads," but such as priests are loth to hear. And we see Sir David Lindsay, the herald, the poet, the King's friend, scourging the lives and sometimes the beliefs of the clergy with verses which rich and poor will know by heart. In short, there was combustible material lying about in large quantities, and sparks were flying.

But the day of revolt was long delayed. What held in check the rebellious and even the Reforming forces, was the best of Scottish traditions, the undying distrust of an England which claimed an overlordship ; and in the days of Henry VIII no wholesomer tradition could there be. His father had schemed for amity by way of matrimonial alliance, and Margaret Tudor had become the wife and mother of Scottish Kings. It was plain that in the age of great monarchies England would be feeble so long as she had a hostile Scotland behind her. But the Tudor would not see that he could not annex Scotland, or that a merely annexed Scotland would still be the old enemy. Just as in the days of the Great Schism England had acknowledged one, and Scotland the other, of the rival Popes, so in the new days of a greater schism James V became the better Catholic because his bullying uncle had broken with Rome. As was natural for a King of Scots, he leant upon the support of the clergy, and thereby he offended his barons. They failed him in his hour of need. After the shameful rout at Solway Moss, he turned his face to the wall and died, a worn-out desperate man at the age of thirty years (December 14, 1542).

His wife, Mary of Lorraine, the sister of those Guises who were to be all-powerful in France, had just borne him a daughter : she was the ill-fated Mary Stewart (December 8, 1542). Once more, a baby was to be crowned in Scotland. Next to her in hereditary succession stood a remote cousin, the head of the House of Hamilton, James Earl of Arran, the Châtelherault of after times. But his right depended on the validity of a divorce which some might call in question ; and Matthew Stewart, Earl of Lennox, had pretensions. At the head of the Scottish clergy stood the able, though dissolute, Archbishop of St Andrews, Cardinal David Beton. For a moment it seemed as if a Reformed religion, or some northern version of Henricanism, was to have its chance. The nobles chose Arran for Regent; many of them envied the clergy; many were in Henry's pay. Arran for a while inclined towards England; he kept heretical chaplains; a Parliament, in spite of clerical protest, declared that the Bible might be read in the vulgar tongue. Beton had been imprisoned; a charge of falsifying the late King's will had been brought against him. Henry's opportunity had come: the little Queen was to be wedded to Edward Tudor. But Henry was the worst of unionists. He bribed, but he also blustered, and let all men see that Scotland must be his by foul means if not by fair. A treaty was signed (July 1, 1543); but within six months (December 11) it was repudiated by the Scots. Meanwhile the feeble Arran, under pressure of an interdict, had reconciled himself with Beton and had abjured his heresies. The old league with France was re-established. Henry then sent fleet and army. Edinburgh was burnt (May, 1544). The Lowlands were ravaged with pitiless ferocity. The Scottish resistance was feeble. There were many traitors. The powerful Douglases played a double part. Lennox was for the English, and was rewarded with the hand of Henry's niece, Margaret Douglas. But Scotland could not be annexed, the precious child could not be captured, and Henry could not yet procure the murder of the Cardinal.

Patriotism and Catholicism were now all one. Not but that there were Protestants. One George Wishart, who had been in Switzerland and at Cambridge, was preaching the Gospel, and some (but this is no better than a guess) would identify him with a Wishart who was plotting Beton's murder. He had powerful protectors, and among his disciples was a man of middle age, born in 1505, who as yet had done nothing memorable; he was priest, notary, private tutor; his name was John Knox. Wishart was arrested, tried and burnt for heresy (March 2, 1546). Thereupon a band of assassins burst into the castle of St Andrews and slew Beton (May 29, 1546). The leaders were well born men, Leslies, Kirkaldys, Melvilles. Their motives were various. Ancient feuds and hopes of English gold were mingled with hatred for a " bloody butcher of the saints of God." They held the castle and the town. The ruffianly and the godly flocked in. There was a strange mixture of debauchery and gospel in the St Andrews of those days. John Knox appeared there and was " called " to preach to the congregation; reluctantly (so he says) he accepted the call. The Regent had laid siege, but had failed. At length came French ships with requisite artillery. The besieged capitulated (July, 1547); they were to be taken to France and there liberated. John Knox was shipped off with the rest, and was kept in the galleys for nineteen months, to meditate on faith that justifies.

Meanwhile Henry of England had died (January 28, 1547); but the Protector Somerset was bent on marrying his boy King to the girl Queen. He had excellent projects in his head. He could speak of a time when England and Scotland would be absorbed and forgotten in Great Britain; but the French also were busy around Mary Stewart. So he led an army northwards, and fought the battle of Pinkie (September 10,

1547). No more decisive defeat could have been inflicted on the Scottish host and the Britannic idea. Other events called Somerset home. The Scots could always be crushed in the field, but Scotland could not be annexed. Then came help from the good friend France, in the shape of French, German, and Italian troops; the English employed Germans and Spaniards. A Parliament decided to accept a French proposal (July, 1548): the Queen of Scots should marry, not the English King, but young Francis the Dauphin, and meantime should be placed out of harm's way. She was shipped off at Dumbarton, and landed in Britanny (August 13, 1548) to pass a happy girlhood in a lettered and luxurious Court. The war was prosecuted with a bloodthirst new in the savage annals of the borders; it was a war fought by mercenary Almains. When peace was signed in 1550, England had gained nothing, and upon the surface (though only upon the surface) Scotland was as Catholic as ever it had been, grateful to France, bitterly resentful against heretical England.

During the struggle Mary of Lorraine had borne herself bravely; she appeared as the guiding spirit of a national resistance. She or her advising kinsfolk were soon to make, though in less brutal sort, the mistake that Henry VIII had made, and this time it was to be irretrievable. During a visit to France (September, 1550—October, 1551) she schemed with her brothers and the French King. She was to take Arran's place as Regent; he had been compensated with the duchy (no empty title) of Châtelherault, and his eldest son (who now becomes the Arran of our story) was to command the French King's Scots guard. The arrangement was not perfected until 1554, for " the second person in the kingdom " was loth to relax his hold on a land of which he might soon be King; but the French influence was strong, and he yielded. Mary of Lorraine was no bad ruler for Scotland; but still the Scots could not help seeing that she was ruling in the interest of a foreign Power. Moreover, there had been a change in the religious environment: Mary Tudor had become Queen of England (July 6, 1553). John Knox, who after his sojourn in the French galleys had been one of King Edward's select preachers and had narrowly escaped the bishopric of Rochester, was fleeing to Geneva; and thence he went to Frankfort, there to quarrel with his fellow exile Dr Cox over the Book of Common Prayer. In Scotland Catholicism had been closely allied with patriotism; but when England became Catholic, Protestant preachers found refuge in Scotland. The King of France was cherishing the intrigues of English heretics against the Spanish Queen; Mary of Lorraine was no fanatic, and her policy was incompatible with stern repression. She was trying to make Scotland more securely French; the task was delicate; and she needed the support of nobles who had little love for the clergy. A few high offices were given to Frenchmen; a few French soldiers were kept in the fortresses; they were few, but enough to scatter whole hosts of undrilled Scots. An attempt to impose a tax for the support of troops was resisted, and the barons showed a strange reluctance to fight the English. At length the time came for the Queen's marriage (April 24, 1558). The Scottish statesmen had laboriously drawn a treaty which should guard the independence of their realm and the rights of the House of Hamilton. This was signed; but a few days earlier Mary Stewart had set her hand to other documents which purported to convey Scotland for good and all to the King of France. We may find excuses for the girl; but, if treason can be committed by a sovereign, she was a traitor. She had treated Scotland as a chattel. The act was secret, but the Scots guessed much and were uneasy.

In the meantime Calvinism, for it was Calvinism now, was spreading. After the quarrels at Frankfort, Knox had gone back to Geneva and had sat at the master's feet. In 1555 he returned to Scotland, no mere preacher, but an organiser also. He went through the country, and "Churches" of the new order sprang into being where he went. Powerful nobles began to listen, such as Lord Lorne, who was soon to be Earl of Argyll, and the Queen's bastard brother, the Lord James Stewart, who was to be Earl of Moray and Regent. And politicians listened also, such as William Maitland, the young laird of Lethington. Knox was summoned before an ecclesiastical Court (May 15, 1556); but apparently at the last moment the hearts of the clergy failed them, and the prosecution was abandoned. It was evident that he had powerful supporters, especially the Earl of Glencairn. Moreover the natural leader of the clergy, John Hamilton, the Primate of Scotland, was a bastard brother of Châtelherault and, as a Hamilton, looked with suspicion on the French policy of Mary of Lorraine, so that the chiefs of Church and State were not united. However, Knox had no mind for martyrdom; and so, after sending to the Regent an admonitory letter, which she cast aside with scornful words, he again departed for Geneva (July, 1556). Then the Bishops summoned him once more; but only his effigy could be burnt.

The preaching went on. In the last days of 1557 the first "Covenant" was signed. "The Congregation of Jesus Christ," of which Argyll, Glencairn, and other great men were members, stood out in undisguised hostility to that "congregation of Satan" which styled itself the Catholic Church. They demanded that King Edward's Prayer Book (which was good enough for them if not for their absent inspirer) should be read in all the churches. The Regent was perplexed; the French marriage had not yet been secured; but she did not prevent the prelates from burning one Walter Milne, who was over eighty years of age (April, 1558). He was the last of the Protestant martyrs; they had not been numerous, even when judged by the modest English standard; fanaticism was not among the many faults of the Scottish prelates; but for this reason his cruel death made the deeper mark. On St Giles' day (September 1) in 1558 that Saint's statue was being carried through

the town of Edinburgh, of which he was the patron.   Under the eyes of
the Regent the priests were rabbled and the idol was smashed in pieces.
It was plain that the next year would be stormy ; and at this crisis the
face of England was once more changed.

A few weeks later Henry Percy, brother of the Earl of Northumberland, was talking with the Duke of Châtelherault.   God, said the
Englishman, has sent you a true and Christian religion.   We are on the
point of receiving the same boon.   Why should you and we be enemies—
we who are hardly out of our servitude to Spain ; you who are being
brought into servitude by France?   The liberties of Scotland are in
jeopardy and the rights of the Hamiltons.   Might we not unite in the
maintenance of God's Word and national independence?   This is the
ideal which springs to light in the last months of 1558 :—deliverance
from the toils of foreign potentates ; amity between two sister nations ;
union in a pure religion.   The Duke himself was a waverer ; his duchy
lay in France ; he is the Antoine de Bourbon of Scottish history ; but
his son the Earl of Arran had lately installed a Protestant preacher at
Châtelherault and was in correspondence with Calvin.   Percy reported
this interview to an English lady who had once been offered to the Duke
as a bride for Arran and had just become Queen Elizabeth.

Mary, Queen of England and Spain, died on the 17th of November,
1558.   The young woman at Hatfield, who knew that her sister's days
were numbered, had made the great choice.   Ever since May it had
been clear that she would soon be Queen.   The Catholics doubted and
feared, but had no other candidate ; King Philip was hopeful.   So
Elizabeth was prepared.   William Cecil was to be her secretary, and
England was to be Protestant.   Her choice may surprise us.   When a
few months later she is told by the Bishop of Aquila that she has been
imprudent, he seems for once to be telling the truth.

Had there been no religious dissension, her title to the throne would
hardly have been contested among Englishmen.   To say nothing of her
father's will, she had an unrepealed statute in her favour.   Divines
and lawyers might indeed have found it difficult to maintain her legitimate birth.   Parliament had lately declared that her father was lawfully
married to Catharine of Aragon, and with this good Catholics would
agree.   But there was another scandal, of which good Protestants might
take account.   Elizabeth's godfather, the Henrican Archbishop and
Protestant martyr, had adjudged that Henry was never married to Anne
Boleyn.   His reasons died with him ; but something bad, something
nameless, might be guessed.   It is sometimes said that Elizabeth's
birth condemned her to be Protestant or bastard.   But it would be
truer to say that, had she cared much about legitimacy, she would have
made her peace with Rome.   Hints came to her thence, that the plenitude of power can set these little matters straight for the benefit of well

disposed princes; and in papal eyes Cranmer's sentence would have been a prejudice in her favour. But pure legitimism, the legitimism of the divine entail, was yet in its infancy, and neither Protestant nor Catholic was bound to deny that a statute of the realm may set a bastard on the throne of William the Conqueror. For the people at large it would be enough that the Lady Elizabeth was the only living descendant of old King Henry, and that beyond her lay civil war. The thin stream of Tudor blood was running dry. Henry's will (but its validity might be questioned) had postponed the issue of his elder to that of his younger sister: in other words, the House of Scotland to the House of Suffolk. Mary Stewart was born in Scotland; she could not have inherited an acre of English land, and it was highly doubtful whether English law would give the crown to an alien who was the child of two aliens. Neither her grandmother's second marriage, namely that with Archibald Douglas (whence sprang Lady Lennox and her son Lord Darnley), nor the marriage of Mary Tudor with Charles Brandon (whence sprang Greys and Stanleys) was beyond reproach;—few marriages were beyond reproach in those days of loose morals and conniving law. John Knox at Geneva had, to Calvin's regret, just blown a first blast of the trumpet against the monstrous regiment of women, and unfortunately, though the tone was new, the tune was not. The Scottish gospeller could only repeat the biblical and other arguments that had been used a century ago by that Lancastrian sage, Chief Justice Fortescue. No woman had sat upon the English throne, save Mary, and she (it might be said) was a statutory Queen. Many people thought that next in right to Elizabeth stood Henry Hastings, who was no Tudor but a Yorkist; and already in 1565 Philip of Spain was thinking of his own descent from Edward III. Thus Elizabeth's statutory title stood between England and wars of the roses which would also be wars of religion.

At this moment, however, she put a difference of creed between herself and the Dauphiness. It may be that in any case Henry II of France, who was in want of arguments for the retention of Calais, would have disputed Elizabeth's legitimacy; it was said that he had been prepared to dispute the legitimacy of her Catholic sister. But had Elizabeth been Catholic, the French and Scottish claim to her throne would have merely been an enemy's insult: an insult to England, a challenge to Spain. As it was, Henry might lay a strong case before the Pope and the Catholic world: Elizabeth was bastard and heretic to boot, and at this moment Paul IV was questioning Ferdinand's election to the Empire because some of his Electors were Lutherans. That heretics are not to rule was no new principle; the Counts of Toulouse had felt its edge in the old Albigensian days.

After the fall of Calais in January (1558) England was panic-stricken. The French were coming; the Scots were coming; Danes and Hanseats were coming. German troops were being hastily hired to protect

Northumberland. Philip's envoy, the Count of Feria, saw incompetence everywhere. The nobles held aloof, while some aged clergymen tried to conduct a war. He hardly dared to think what would happen if a few French ships touched the shore. Since then, there had been some improvement. No invader had landed, and Guise's capture of Thionville had been balanced by Egmont's victory at Gravelines. Shortly before Mary's death negotiations for a peace were begun at Cercamp; the outline of the scheme was a restoration of conquests. But Calais stopped the way. The French could not surrender that prize, and they were the more constant in their determination because the King of Spain would not much longer be King of England, and an isolated England would have no conquest to restore. When Elizabeth became Queen, Calais was not yet lost; that was the worst of it. Both Kings were weary of the war; behind both yawned gulfs of debt and heresy. But the ruler of the Netherlands was deeply concerned in the recovery of Calais—perhaps more materially, though less sentimentally, than were the English. Feria has reported the profound remark that when Calais was captured many Englishmen ceased to go to church. A Protestant Elizabeth might have to sign away the last memorial of old glories; and that would not fill the churches. Philip, it might be plain, would not suffer the French to invade England through Scotland; but the tie between Spain and an heretical England would be the coolest selfishness, the King's mind would be distracted between his faith and his policy, and if he were compelled to save England from the French, he certainly would not save England for the English.

True that for Protestant eyes there was light on the horizon. Anyone could see that there would be religious troubles in France and Scotland. Geneva was active, and Rome seemed to be doting. That summer the psalms had gone up loudly from the Pré-aux-Clercs, and a Châtillon had been arrested. That autumn St Giles of Edinburgh had lain prostrate in the mud. Expectant heirs and royal cadets, Bourbons and Hamiltons, were wavering; Maximilian was listening to an enlightened pastor; France, Scotland, the Empire, might some day fall to evangelical lords. Good news came from Poland, Bohemia, and Hungary; it was even rumoured that the Pope would at last succeed in shaking Philip's faith. Still, the black fact of the moment was that Philip and Henry were making peace in order that they might crush their respective heretics. And England's military weakness was patent to all. Her soldiers and captains were disgracefully old-fashioned, and what gunpowder she had was imported from the Netherlands. "To make a lewd comparison," said an Englishman, "England is as a bone thrown between two dogs." Was this bone to display an irritating activity of its own, merely because the two dogs seemed for the moment to be equal and opposite? To more than one mind came the same thought: "They will make a Piedmont of England."

Within the country the prospect was dubious. The people were discontented: defeat and shame, pestilence and famine had lately been their lot. A new experiment would be welcome; but it would miserably fail were it not speedily successful. No doubt, the fires in Smithfield had harmed the Catholic cause by confirming the faith and exasperating the passions of the Protestants. No doubt, the Spanish marriage was detested. But we may overestimate the dislike of persecution and the dislike of Spain. No considerable body of Englishmen would deny that obstinate heretics should be burnt. There was no need for Elizabeth to marry Philip or bring Spaniards into the land; but the Spanish alliance, the old Anglo-Burgundian alliance, was highly valued: it meant safety and trade and occasional victories over the hereditary foe. Moreover, the English Reformers were without a chief; beyond Elizabeth they had no pretender to the throne; they had no apostle, no prophet; they were scattered over Europe and had been quarrelling, Knoxians against Coxians, in their foreign abodes. Edward's reign had worn the gloss off the new theology. We may indeed be sure that, had Elizabeth adhered to the old faith, she must have quelled plots and rebellions or herself been quelled. We look at Scotland, France, and the Netherlands, and, it may be, infer that the storm would have overwhelmed her. Perhaps we forget how largely the tempests that we see elsewhere were due to the momentous choice that she made for England. It must probably be allowed that most of the young men of brains and energy who grew to manhood under Mary were lapsing from Catholicism, and that the educated women were falling faster and further. London too, Bonner's London, was Protestant, and London might be worth an abolished Mass. But when, after some years of fortunate and dexterous government, we see how strong is the old creed, how dangerous is Mary Stewart as its champion, we cannot feel sure that Elizabeth chose the path which was, or which seemed to be, the safest.

Of her own opinions she told strange tales. Puzzled by her shifty discourse, a Spanish envoy once suggested atheism. When a legal settlement had been made, it was her pleasure, and perhaps her duty, to explain that her religion was that of all sensible people. The difference between the various versions of Christianity " *n'estoit que bagatelle.*" So she agreed with the Pope, except about some details; she cherished the Augsburg confession, or something very like it; she was at one, or nearly at one, with the Huguenots. She may have promised her sister (but this is not proved) to make no change in religion; at any rate she had gone to mass without much ado. Nevertheless it is not unlikely that at the critical time her conduct was swayed rather by her religious beliefs or disbeliefs than by any close calculation of loss and gain. She had not her father's taste for theology; she was neither prig like her brother nor zealot like her sister; but she had been taught from the first to contemn the Pope, and during Edward's reign she had been highly educated in the newest doctrines. John Hooper, the father of the Puritans, had admired her displays of argumentative divinity. More than one Catholic who spoke with her in later days was struck by her ignorance of Catholic verity. The Bishop of Aquila traced her phrases to " the heretic Italian friars." He seems to have been thinking of Vermigli and Ochino, and there may have been some little truth in his guess. Once she said that she liked Italian ways and manners better than any other, and sometimes seemed to herself half Italian. Her eyes filled with tears over Peter Martyr's congratulations. She had talked predestination with Fra Bernardino and had translated one of his sermons ; the Puritans were persuaded that if she would listen to no one else, she would listen to him. All this might have meant little ; but then she had suffered in the good cause. She had been bullied into going to mass ; she had been imprisoned ; she had nearly been excluded from the throne ; some ardent Catholics had sought her life ; and her suspected heresies had been at least a part of her offending. It would have been base to disappoint all those who had prayed for her and plotted for her, and pleasant it was when from many lands came letters which hailed her as the miraculously preserved champion of the truth. She had a text ready for the bearer of the good news : " This is the Lord's doing and it is marvellous in our eyes."

One point was clear. The Henrican Anglo-Catholicism was dead and buried. It died with Henry and was interred by Stephen Gardiner. In distant days its spirit might arise from the tomb ; but not yet. The Count of Feria and Bishop Tunstall were at needless pains to explain to the young Queen that she was favouring "Lutherans and Zwinglians," whom her father would have burnt. But in 1558 nothing was to be gained by mere schism. Her fellow sovereigns, more especially her brother-in-law, could have taught her that a prince might enjoy all the advantages of spotless orthodoxy and yet keep the Pope at arm's length. Many Englishmen hated " popery"; but by this time the core of the popery that they hated was no longer the Papacy, but the idolatrous Mass. The choice lay between Catholicism with its Pope and the creed for which Cranmer and Ridley died. It could scarcely be hoped that the Bishops would yield an inch. Very shame, if no worthier motive, would keep them true to the newly restored supremacy of Rome. Happily for Elizabeth, they were few and feeble. Reginald Pole had hardly outlived Mary, and for one reason or another had made no haste in filling vacant sees ;—Feria thought that the " accursed Cardinal" had French designs. And death had been and still was busy. Only sixteen instead of twenty-six Bishops were entitled to attend the critical Parliament, and only eleven with the Abbot of Westminster were present. Their constancy in the day of trial makes them respectable ; but not one of them was a leader of men. The ablest of them had been Henry's ministers and therefore could be taunted as renegades.

A story which came from a good quarter bade us see Elizabeth announcing to the Pope her accession to the throne, and not rejecting Catholicism until Paul IV declared that England was a papal fief and she an usurping bastard. Now, Caraffa was capable of any imprudence and just at this moment seemed bent on reviving the claims of medieval Pontiffs, in order that he might drive a long-suffering Emperor into the arms of the Lutherans. But it is certain now that in the matter of courtesy Elizabeth, not Paul, was the offender. She ignored his existence. Edward Carne was living at Rome as Mary's ambassador. He received no letters of credence from the new Queen, and on the 1st of February, 1559, she told him to come home as she had nothing for him to do. Meanwhile the French were thinking to obtain a Bull against her; they hoped that at all events Paul would not allow her to marry her dead sister's husband. At Christmastide (1558), when she was making a scene in her chapel over the elevation of the Host, the Pope was talking kindly of her to the French ambassador, would not promise to refuse a dispensation, but could not believe that another Englishwoman would want to marry a detestable Spaniard. A little later he knew more about her and detained Carne (a not unwilling prisoner) at Rome (March 27), not because she was base-born, but because she had revolted from the Holy See. He had just taken occasion to declare in a Bull that princes guilty of heresy are deprived of all lawful power by the mere fact of their guilt (February 15). This edict, though it may have been mainly aimed at Ferdinand's three Protestant Electors, was a salutary warning for Elizabeth and Anthony and Maximilian; but no names were named. Philip had influence enough to balk the French intrigue and protect his sister-in-law from a direct anathema. The Spaniard may in Paul's eyes have been somewhat worse than a heretic; but the quarrel with the other Habsburg, and then the sudden attack upon his own scandalous nephews, were enough to consume the few remaining days of the fierce old man. He has much to answer for; but it was no insult from him that made Elizabeth a Protestant.

No time was lost. Mary's death (November 17, 1558) dissolved a Parliament. Heath, Archbishop of York and Chancellor of the realm, dismissed it, and with loyal words proclaimed the new Queen. Within three weeks (December 5) writs went out for a new Parliament. Elizabeth was going to exact conformity to a statutory religion. For the moment the statutory religion was the Roman Catholic, and she would have taken a false step if in the name of some higher law she had annulled or ignored the Marian statutes. At once she forbade innovations and thus disappointed the French who hoped for a turbulent revolution. A new and happy *et caetera* was introduced into the royal style and seemed to hint, without naming, a Headship of the Church. Every change pointed one way. Some of the old Councillors were retained, but the new Councillors were Protestants. William Cecil, then

aged thirty-eight, had been Somerset's and was to be Elizabeth's secretary. Like her he had gone to mass, but no Catholic doubted that he
was a sad heretic. The Great Seal, resigned by Heath, was given to
Nicholas Bacon. He and Cecil had married sisters who were godly
ladies of the new sort. The imprisoned heretics were bailed, and the
refugees flocked back from Frankfort, Zurich and Geneva. Hardly was
Mary dead, before one Bishop was arrested for an inopportune sermon
(November 27). Another preached at her funeral (December 13) and
praised her for rejecting that title which Elizabeth had not yet assumed ;
he too was put under restraint. Mary's chief mourner was not her sister,
but, appropriately enough, the Lady Lennox who was to have supplanted
Elizabeth. No Bishop preached the funeral sermon for Charles V, and
what good could be said of that Catholic Caesar was said by the
Protestant Dr Bill (December 24). The new Queen was artist to the
finger-tips. The English Bible was rapturously kissed ; the Tower
could not be re-entered without uplifted eyes and thankful words ; her
hand (it was a pretty hand) shrank, so folk said, from Bonner's lips.
Christmas-day was chosen for a more decisive scene. The Bishop who
was to say mass in her presence was told not to elevate the Host. He
would not obey ; so after the Gospel out went Elizabeth ; she could no
longer witness that idolatry. Three weeks later (January 15) she was
crowned while Calvin was dedicating to her his comments on Isaiah.
What happened at the coronation is obscure. The Bishops, it seems,
swore fealty in the accustomed manner; the Epistle and Gospel were read
in English; it is said that the celebrant was one of the Queen's chaplains
and that he did not elevate the Host; it is said that she did not com-
municate ; she was anointed by the Bishop of Carlisle, whose rank
would not have entitled him to this office, had not others refused it.
At length the day came for a Parliament (January 25). A mass was
said at Westminster early in the morning. At a later hour the Queen
approached the Abbey with her choir singing in English. The last
of the Abbots came to meet her with monks and candles. " Away
with those torches " she exclaimed : " we can see well enough ! " And
then Edward's tutor, Dr Cox, late of Frankfort, preached ; and he
preached, it is said, for an hour and a half, the peers all standing.

The negotiations between Spain, England and France had been
brought to a pause by Mary's death, but were to be resumed after a
brief interval, during which Elizabeth was to make up her mind. Some
outwardly amicable letters passed between her and Henry II. She tried
to play the part of the pure-bred Englishwoman, who should not suffer
for the sins of the Spanish Mary. But the French were not to be coaxed
out of Calais, and she knew that they were seeking a papal Bull against
her. It became plain that she must not detach herself from Spain and
that, even with Philip's help, Calais could only be obtained after another
war, for which England was shamefully unready. Then, in the middle of

January, came through Feria the expected offer of Philip's hand. Elizabeth seemed to hesitate, had doubts about the Pope's dispensing power and so forth; but in the end said that she did not mean to marry, and added that she was a heretic. Philip, it seems, was relieved by the refusal; he had laboriously explained to his ambassador that his proposal was a sacrifice laid upon the altar of the Catholic faith. He had hopes, which were encouraged in England, that one of his Austrian cousins, Ferdinand or Charles, would succeed where he had failed, secure England for orthodoxy, and protect the Netherlands from the ill example that an heretical England would set.

Meanwhile the great Treaty of Cateau-Cambrésis was in the making. Elizabeth tried to retain Philip's self-interested support; and she retained it. Without substantial aid from England, he would not fight for Calais; she would have to sign it away; but so earnest had he been in this matter that the French covenanted to restore the treasured town after eight years and further to pay half-a-million of crowns by way of penalty in case they broke their promise. No one supposed that they would keep it; still they had consented to make the retention of Calais a just cause for war, and Elizabeth could plausibly say that some remnants of honour had been saved. But the clouds collected once more. New differences broke out among the negotiators, who had half a world to regulate, and, before the intricate settlement could be completed, a marriage had been arranged between Philip and one of Henry's daughters. Elizabeth of France, not Elizabeth of England, was to be the bride. The conjunction was ominous for heretics.

From the first days of February to the first days of April the negotiations had been pending. Meanwhile in England little had been accomplished. It had become plain that the clergy in possession (but there was another and expectant clergy out of possession) would not yield. The Convocation of Canterbury met when Parliament met, and the Lower House declared for transubstantiation, the sacrifice of the Mass, and the Roman supremacy; also it idly protested that laymen were not to meddle with faith, worship, or discipline (February 17, 1559). The Bishops were staunch; the English Church by its constitutional organs refused to reform itself; the Reformation would be an unprecedented state-stroke. Probably the assembled Commons were willing to strike. The influence of the Crown had been used on the Protestant side; but Cecil had hardly gathered the reins in his hand and the government's control over the electoral machinery must have been unusually weak. Our statistics are imperfect, but the number of knights and burgesses who, having served in 1558, were again returned in 1559 was not abnormally small, and with the House of 1558 Mary had been well content. Also we may see at Westminster not a few men who soon afterwards are "hinderers of true religion" or at best only "faint professors"; but probably the nation at large was not unwilling that

Elizabeth should make her experiment. A few creations and restorations of peerages strengthened the Protestant element among the lords. The Earl of Bedford and Lord Clinton appeared as proxies for many absent peers, and, of all the lords, Bedford (Francis Russell) was the most decisively committed to radical reform. The Howards were for the Queen, their cousin; the young Duke of Norfolk, England's one duke, was at this time ardently Protestant, and in the next year was shocked at the sight of undestroyed altars.

Money was cheerfully voted. The Queen was asked to choose a husband, and professed her wish to die a maid. She may have meant what she said, but assuredly did not mean that it should be believed. A prudently phrased statute announced that she was "lawfully descended and come of the blood royal"; another declared her capable of inheriting from her divorced and attainted mother; the painful past was veiled in general words. There was little difficulty about a resumption of those tenths and first-fruits which Mary had abandoned. Round the question of ecclesiastical supremacy the battle raged, and it raged for two months and more (February 9 to April 29). Seemingly the Queen's ministers carried through the Lower House a bill which went the full Henrican length in its Caesaro-papalism and its severity. Upon pain of a traitor's death, everyone was to swear that Elizabeth was the Supreme Head of the Church of England. In the Upper House, to which the bill came on the 27th of February, the Bishops had to oppose a measure which would leave the lives of all open Romanists at the mercy of the government. Few though they were, the dozen prelates could still do much in a House where there were rarely more than thirty temporal lords, and probably Cecil had asked for more than he wanted. On the 18th of March the project had taken a far milder form; forfeiture of office and benefice was to be the punishment of those who would not swear. Against this more lenient measure only two temporal lords protested; but a Catholic says that other "good Christians" were feigning to be ill. The bill went back to the Commons; then back with amendments to the Lords, who read it thrice on the 22nd. Easter fell on the 26th, and it had been hoped that by that time Parliament would have finished its work. Very little had been done; doctrine and worship had hardly been touched. Apparently an attempt to change the services of the Church had been made, had met with resistance, and had been abandoned.

Elizabeth was in advance of the law and beckoned the nation forward. During that Lent the Court sermon had been the only sermon, the preacher Scory or Sandys, Grindal or Cox. A papist's excited fancy saw a congregation of five thousand and heard extravagant blasphemy. On Easter day the Queen received the Communion in both kinds; the news ran over Europe; Antoine de Bourbon on the same day had done the like at Pau; Mary of Lorraine had marked that festival for the return of all Scots to the Catholic worship. The colloquy of Westminster follows. There was to be a trial by battle in the Abbey between chosen champions of the two faiths. Its outcome might make us suspect that a trap was laid by the Protestants. But it is by no means certain that the challenge came from their side, and the Spanish ambassador took some credit for arranging the combat. The colloquy of Westminster stands midway between that of Worms (1557) and that of Poissy (1561). The Catholics were wont to get the better in these feats of arms, because, so soon as Christ's presence in the Eucharist was mentioned, the Protestants fell a-fighting among themselves. Apparently on this occasion the rules of the debate were settled by Heath and Bacon. The Great Seal had passed from an amiable to an abler keeper. The men of the Old Learning were to defend the use of Latin in the services of the Church, to deny that a " particular Church " can change rites and ceremonies and to maintain the propitiatory sacrifice of the Mass. Their first two theses would bring them into conflict with national feeling ; and at the third point they would be exposed to the united force of Lutherans and Helvetians, for the sacrifice, and not the presence, was to be debated. It was a less advantage for the Reformers that their adversaries were to speak first, for there was to be no extemporary argument but only a reading of written dissertations. In the choir of the abbey, before Council, Lords, Commons and multitude, the combatants took their places on Friday, the 31st of March. At once the Catholics began to except against the rules that they were required to observe. Dr Cole, however, maintained their first proposition and Dr Horne read the Protestant essay. The Reformers were well content with that day's work and the applause that followed. On Monday the second question was to be handled. Of what happened we have no impartial account ; we do not know what had passed between Heath and Bacon, or whether the Catholic doctors were taken by surprise. Howbeit, they chose the worst course ; they wrangled about procedure and refused to continue the debate. Apparently they were out of heart and leaderless. Two of the Bishops were forthwith imprisoned by the Council for intemperate words, and thus the Catholic party in the House of Lords was seriously weakened at a critical moment. Moreover, the inference that men do not break off a debate with preliminary objections when they are confident of success in the main issue, though it is not always just, is always natural.

The next day Parliament resumed its work. Meanwhile, Elizabeth had at length decided that she would not assume the Henrican title, though assuredly she had meant that it should be, as it had been, offered to her. Women should keep silence in the churches ; so there was difficulty about a " dumb head." She had managed to get a little credit from Philip's envoy and a little from zealous Calvinists by saying that she would not be Head of the Church, and she could then tell appropriate persons that she scorned a style which the Pope had polluted. So Cecil had to go to the Commons and explain that there must be a new bill and new oath. He met with some opposition, for there were who held that the Queen was Supreme Head *iure divino*. Ultimately a phrase was fashioned which declared that she was the only Supreme Governor of the realm as well in all spiritual or ecclesiastical things or causes as in temporal, and that no foreign prince or prelate had any ecclesiastical or spiritual authority within her dominions. However, among other statutes of Henry VIII, one was revived which proclaims that the King is Head of the Church, and that by the word of God all ecclesiastical jurisdiction flows from him. Catholics suspected that Elizabeth's husband would be head of the Church, if not head of his wife, and saw the old title concealed behind the new *et caetera*. Protestant lawyers said that she could take the title whenever she pleased. Sensible men saw that, having the substance, she could afford to waive the irritating name. On the 14th of April the bill was before the Lords. There were renewed debates and more changes; and the famous Act of Supremacy was not finally secured until the 29th.

In the last days of an unusually long session a bill for the Uniformity of Religion went rapidly through both Houses (April 18–28). The services prescribed in a certain Book of Common Prayer, and none other, were to be lawful. The embryonic history of this measure is obscure. An informal committee of Protestant divines seems to have been appointed by the Queen to prepare a book. It has been thought that as the basis of their labours they took the Second Book of Edward VI, but desired a further simplification of ceremonies. On the other hand, there are some signs that Cecil and the Queen thought that the Second Book, which had hardly been introduced before it was abrogated, had already gone far enough or too far in the abolition of accustomed rites. All this, however, is very uncertain. Our guess may be that, when men were weary of the prolonged debate over the Supremacy and its continuance was becoming a national danger (for violent speeches had been made), the Queen's advisers took the short course of proposing the Book of 1552 with very few changes. At such a moment relief might be found in what could be called a mere act of restoration, and the Edwardian Book, however unfamiliar, was already ennobled by the blood of martyrs. There are signs of haste, or of divided counsels, for the new Book when it came from the press differed in some little, but not trivial, matters from that which Parliament had expressly sanctioned. The changes sanctioned by Parliament were few. An offensive phrase about the Bishop of Rome's "detestable enormities" was expunged, apparently by the House of Lords. An addition from older sources was made to the words that accompany the delivery of bread and wine to the communicant, whereby a charge of the purest Zwinglianism might be obviated. At the moment it was of importance to Elizabeth that she should assure the German Princes that her religion was

Augustan; for they feared, and not without cause, that it was Helvetian. A certain "black rubric" which had never formed part of the statutory book fell away; it would have offended Lutherans; we have reason to believe that it had been inserted in order to meet the scruples of John Knox. Of what was done in the matter of ornaments by the statute, by the rubrics of the Book and by "injunctions" that the Queen promptly issued, it would be impossible to speak fairly without a lengthy quotation of documents, the import of which became in the nineteenth century a theme of prolonged and inconclusive disputation. It must here suffice that there are few signs of any of the clergymen who accepted the Prayer Book either having worn or having desired to wear in the ordinary churches—there was at times a little more splendour in cathedrals—any ecclesiastical robe except the surplice. But, to return to Elizabeth's Parliament, we have it on fairly good authority that nine temporal lords, including the Treasurer (the Marquis of Winchester), and nine prelates (two Bishops were in gaol) voted against the bill, and that it was only carried by three votes. Unfortunately at an exciting moment there is a gap, perhaps a significant gap, in the official record, and we cease to know what lords were present in the house. But about thirty temporal peers had lately been in attendance, and so we may infer that some of them were inclined neither to alter the religion of England nor yet to oppose the Queen. On the 5th of May, the Bishops were fighting in vain for the renovated monasteries. On the 8th, Parliament was dissolved.

At a moment of strain and peril a wonderfully durable settlement had been made. There is cause for thinking that the Queen's advisers had been compelled to abandon considerable parts of a lengthy programme; but the great lines had been drawn and were permanent. For this reason they can hardly be described in words that are both just and few; but perhaps we may make a summary of those points which were the most important to the men of 1559. A radical change in doctrine, worship and discipline has been made by Queen and Parliament against the will of prelates and ecclesiastical Councils. The legislative power of the Convocations is once more subjected to royal control. The derivation of episcopal from royal jurisdiction has been once more asserted in the words of Henry VIII. Appeal from the Courts of the Church lies to royal delegates who may be laymen. What might fairly be called a plenitude of ecclesiastical jurisdiction of the corrective sort can be, and at once is, committed to delegates who constitute what is soon known as the Court of High Commission and strongly resembles the consistory of a German Prince. Obstinate heresy is still a capital crime; but practically the Bishops have little power of forcing heretics to stand a trial, and, unless Parliament and Convocation otherwise ordain, only the wilder sectaries will be in danger of burning. There is no "liberty of cult." The Prayer Book prescribes the only lawful form of common worship. The clergyman who adopts any other, even in a private chapel, commits a crime; so does he who procures this aberration from conformity. Everyone must go to church on Sunday and bide prayer and preaching or forfeit twelve pence to the use of the poor. Much also can be done to ensure conformity by excommunication which has imprisonment behind it. The papal authority is abolished. Clergy and office-holders can be required to swear that it is naught; if they refuse the oath, they lose office and benefice. If anyone advisedly maintains that authority, he forfeits his goods; on a third conviction he is a traitor. The service book is not such as will satisfy all ardent Reformers; but their foreign fathers in the faith think it not intolerable, and the glad news goes out that the Mass is abolished. The word " Protestant," which is rapidly spreading from Germany, comes as a welcome name. In the view of an officially inspired apologist of the Elizabethan settlement, those who are not Papists are Protestants.

The requisite laws had been made, but whether they would take effect was very uncertain. The new oath was not tendered to the judges; and some of them were decided Romanists. Nor was the validity of the statutes unquestioned, for it was by no means so plain as it now is that an Act against which the spiritual Lords have voted in a body may still be an Act of the three Estates. Gradually in the summer and autumn the Bishops were called upon to swear; they refused and were deprived. It is not certain that the one weak brother, Kitchin of Llandaff, actually swore the oath, though he promised to exact it from others. Futile hopes seem to have been entertained that Tunstall and Heath would at least take part in the consecration of their Protestant successors. Such successors were nominated by the Queen; but to make Bishops of them was not easy. Apparently a government bill dealing with this matter had come to naught. Probably the Queen's advisers had intended to abolish the canonical election; they procured its abolition in Ireland on the ground that it was inconsistent with the Royal Supremacy; but for some cause or another the English Parliament had restored that grotesque Henrican device, the compulsory election of a royal nominee. By a personal interview Elizabeth secured the conversion of the dean of the two metropolitan churches, that pliant old diplomat Nicholas Wotton. When sees and benefices were rapidly falling vacant, his adhesion was of great importance if all was to be done in an orderly way.

But given the election, there must still be confirmation and consecration; statute required it. The cooperation of four " Bishops " would be necessary if Matthew Parker was to sit where Reginald Pole had sat. Four men in episcopal Orders might be found: for instance, William Barlow, of whose Protestant religion there could be no doubt, since Albert of Prussia had lately attested it; but these men would not be in possession of English sees. Moreover, it seems to have been doubted

whether the Edwardian Ordinal had been revived as part of the Edwardian
Prayer Book.   Cecil was puzzled, but equal to the occasion.   In a docu-
ment redolent of the papal chancery Elizabeth "supplied" all "defects,"
and at length on the 17th of December, in the chapel at Lambeth,
Parker was consecrated with Edwardian rites by Barlow, Scory, Coverdale
and Hodgkin.   The story of a simpler ceremony at the Nag's Head
tavern was not concocted until long afterwards; it should have for
pendants a Protestant fable which told of a dramatic scene between
Elizabeth and the Catholic prelates, and an Anglican fable which strove
to suggest that the Prayer Book was sanctioned by a synod of Bishops
and clergy.   A large number of deans and canons followed the example
set by the Bishops.   Of their inferiors hardly more than two hundred, so
it seems, were deprived for refusing the oath.   The royal commissioners
treated the hesitating priests with patient forbearance; and the meaning
of the oath was minimised by an ably worded Proclamation.   We may
conjecture that many of those who swore expected another turn of
the always turning wheel.   However, Elizabeth succeeded in finding
creditable occupants for the vacant dignities; of Parker and some of his
suffragans more than this might be said.   The new service was introduced without exciting disturbances; the altars and roods were pulled
down, tables were purchased, and a coat of whitewash veiled the pictured
saints from view.   Among the laity there was much despondent in-
difference.   Within a dozen years there had been four great changes
in worship, and no good had come of it all.   For some time afterwards
there are many country gentlemen whom the Bishops describe as
"indifferent in religion."   Would the Queen's Church secure them and
their children?   That question could not be answered by one who
looked only at England.   From the first, Elizabeth and Cecil, who
were entering into their long partnership, had looked abroad.

The month of May, 1559, which saw the ratification of the Treaty
of Cateau-Cambrésis, is a grand month in the annals of the heresy
which was to be destroyed.   A hideous act of faith at Valladolid may show
us that Catholicism is safe in Spain; but the English Parliament ends
its work, a French Reformed Church shapes itself in the synod of Paris,
and Scotland bursts into flame.   In 1558 we saw it glowing.   Mary of
Guise was temporising; she had not yet obtained the crown matrimonial
for the Dauphin.   In the winter Parliament she had her way; the crown
was to be (but never was) carried to her son-in-law.   His father had
just ceased his intrigues with English Protestants, and was making peace
in order that he might be busy among the Protestants of France.   The
Regent of Scotland was given to understand that the time for tolerance
was past.   In March, 1559, the Scottish prelates followed the example of
their English brethren and uttered their *Non possumus*.   They proposed
to remedy many an indefensible abuse, but to new beliefs there could

be no concession. The Queen-mother fixed Easter day for the return of all men to the Catholic worship. The order was disregarded. On the 10th of May the more notorious of the preachers were to answer at Stirling for their misdeeds. They collected at Perth, with Protestant lords around them. At this moment Elizabeth's best friend sprang into the arena. John Knox had been fuming at Dieppe. Elizabeth, enraged at his ill-timed "blast," denied him a safe conduct. François Morel, too, the French Reformer, implored Calvin to keep this fire-brand out of England lest all should be spoilt. But if Knox chose to revisit his native land that was no affair of Elizabeth's, and he was predestinated to win for Calvinism the most durable of its triumphs. He landed in Scotland on the 2nd of May and was at Perth by the 11th. Then there was a sermon; a stone was thrown; an image was broken, and the churches of St Johnston were wrecked. Before the end of the month there were two armed hosts in the field. There were more sermons, and where Knox preached the idols fell and monks and nuns were turned adrift. There were futile negotiations and disregarded truces. At the head of the belligerent Congregation rode Glencairn, Argyll, and Lord James. Châtelherault was still with the Regent; and she had a small force of disciplined Frenchmen. At the end of July a temporary truce was made at Leith. The Congregation could bring a numerous host (of the medieval sort) into the field, but could not keep it there. However, as the power of the French soldiers was displayed, the revolutionary movement became more and more national. The strife, if it was between Catholic and Calvinist, was also a strife for the delivery of Scotland from a foreign army. None the less there was a revolt. Thenceforth, Calvinism often appears as a rebellious religion. This, however, is its first appearance in that character. Calvin had long been a power in the world of Reformed theology, and his death (1564) was not far distant; but in 1559 the Count of Feria was at pains to tell King Philip that "this Calvin is a Frenchman and a great heretic" (March 19). Knox, when he preached "the rascal multitude" into iconoclastic fury was setting an example to *Gueux* and Huguenots. What would Elizabeth think of it?

Throughout the winter and spring Englishmen and Scots, who had been dragged into war by their foreign masters, had been meeting on the border and talking first of armistice and then of peace. Already in January Maitland of Lethington had a strong desire to speak with Sir William Cecil and since then had been twice in London. He was the Regent's Secretary, conforming in religion as Cecil had conformed; but it is likely that the core of such creed as he had was unionism. The news that came from Scotland in May can hardly have surprised the English Secretary. "Some great consequences must needs follow": this was his quiet comment (May 26). Diplomatic relations with France had just been resumed. Nicholas Throckmorton, one of those able men who begin to collect around Elizabeth, had gone to reside there as her ambassador, had gone to " practise " there and exacerbate the " garboils " there. One of the first bits of news that he sends home is that Arran has been summoned to Court from Poitou, where he has been Calvinising, has disobeyed the summons and cannot be found (May 30). The Guises connect Arran's disappearance with Throckmorton's advent; and who shall say that they are wrong? In June Cecil heard from the border that the Scottish lords were devising how this young man could be brought home and married " you know where." " You have a Queen," said a Scot to Throckmorton, " and we our Prince the Earl of Arran, marriable both, and the chief upholders of God's religion." Arran might soon be King of Scotland. The Dauphiness, who at the French Court was being called Queen of England, did not look as if she were long for this world: Throckmorton noted her swoons. Arran had escaped to Geneva. Early in July Elizabeth was busy, and so was Calvin, over the transmission of this invaluable youth to the quarter where he could best serve God and the English Queen. Petitions for aid had come from Scotland. Cecil foresaw what would happen : the Protestants were to be helped " first with promises, next with money, and last with arms " (July 8). But to go beyond the first stage was hazardous. The late King of England was only a few miles off with his fleet and veteran troops ; he was being married by proxy to a French Princess ; he had thoughts of enticing Catharine Grey out of England, in order that he might have another candidate for the throne, if it were necessary to depose the disobedient Elizabeth. And could Elizabeth openly support these rebels ? In the answer to that question lay the rare importance of Arran. The Scottish uproar must become a constitutional movement directed by a prince of the blood royal against a French attempt to deprive a nation of its independence. Cecil explained to Calvin that if true religion is to be supported it must first convert great noblemen (June 22).

Then the danger from France seemed to increase. There was a mischance at a tournament and Henry II was dead (July 10). The next news was that " the House of Guise ruleth" (July 13). In truth, this was good news. Elizabeth's adversary was no longer an united France. The Lorrainers were not France ; their enemies told them that they were not French. But the Duke and Cardinal were ruling France ; they came to power as the uncles of the young King's wife, and soon there might be a boy born who would be Valois-Tudor-Stewart-Guise. A Guise was ruling Scotland also, and the rebellion against her was hanging fire. So early in August Cecil's second stage was reached, and Ralph Sadler was carrying three thousand pounds to the border. He knew his Scotland ; Henry VIII had sent him there on a fool's errand ; there would be better management this time. In the same month Philip turned his back on the Netherlands, never to see them more. Thenceforth, he would be the secluded King of a distant country. Also, Paul IV died, and for four

months the Roman Church had no supreme governor. The Supreme
Governor of the English Church could breathe more freely. She kept
her St Bartholomew (August 24). There was burning in Bartlemy Fair,
burning in Smithfield—but only of wooden roods and Maries and Johns
and such-like popish gear. " It is done of purpose to confirm the
Scottish revolt ": such was a guess made at Brussels (September 2) ; and
it may have been right, for there was little of the natural iconoclast in
Elizabeth. A few days later (August 29) Arran was safely and secretly
in her presence, and thence was smuggled into Scotland. Probably she
took his measure ; he was not quite sane, but would be useful. Soon
afterwards Philip's ambassador knew that she was fomenting tumults
in Scotland through " a heretic preacher called Knox." That was
unkindly said, but not substantially untrue. Early in October " the
Congregation" began once more to take an armed shape. Châtelherault,
that unstable " second person," had been brought over by his impetuous
son. The French troops in Scotland had been reinforced ; the struggle
was between Scot and Frenchman. So, to the horror of Bishops-elect
(whose consecration had not yet been managed), the table in Elizabeth's
chapel began to look like an altar with cross and candles. " She will
not favour the Scots in their religion," said Gilles de Noailles the French
ambassador. " She is afraid," said the Cardinal of Lorraine. " She is
going to marry the Archduke Charles who is coming here in disguise,"
said many people. Surely she wished that just those comments should
be made ; and so Dr Cox, by this time elect of Ely, had to stomach
cross and candles as best he might.

The host of the Congregation arrived at Edinburgh ; a manifesto
declared that the Regent was deposed (October 21). She and the
French were fortifying Leith ; the castle was held by the neutral Lord
Erskine. But once more the extemporised army began to melt away.
Treasure sent by Elizabeth was captured by a border ruffian, James
Hepburn, Earl of Bothwell, who was to play a part in coming tragedies.
The insurgents fled from Edinburgh (November 6). In negotiation
with Cecil, Knox was showing the worldly wisdom that underlay his
Hebraic frenzies ; he knew the weak side of his fellow-countrymen ;
without more aid from England, the movement would fail. Knox,
however, was not presentable at Court ; Lethington was. The Regent's
Secretary had left her and had carried to the opposite camp the state-
craft that it sorely needed. He saw a bright prospect for his native
land and took the road to London. Cecil's third stage was at hand.
There were long debates in the English Council; there were " Philipians"
in it, and all that passed there was soon known at the French embassy.
The Queen was irresolute ; even Bacon was for delay ; but, though some
French ships had been wrecked, others were ready, and the danger to
Scotland, and through Scotland to England, was very grave. At length
Cecil and Lethington won their cause. An army under the Duke of

Norfolk was to be raised and placed on the border. Large supplies of arms had been imported from the dominions of the Catholic King. Bargains for professed soldiers were struck with German princes   William Winter, Master of the Ordnance, was to take fourteen ships to the Forth. He might " as of his own hand" pick a quarrel with the French; but there was to be no avowed war (December 16).   On the morrow Dr Parker was consecrated.   He had been properly shocked by Knox's doings.   " God keep us from such visitation as Knox hath attempted in Scotland: the people to be orderers of things!" (November 6).   If in that autumn the people of Scotland had not ordered things in a summary way, Dr Parker's tenure of the archiepiscopate might have been precarious.   A few days later and there was once more a Pope (December 25): this time a sane Pope, Pius IV, who would have to deplore the loss, not only of England, but of Scotland also.   God of His mercy, said Lethington, had removed that difference of religion.

Once more the waves were kind to Elizabeth.   They repulsed the Marquis of Elbeuf (René of Lorraine), and suffered Winter to pass.   All the news that came from France was good.   It told of unwillingness that national treasure should be spent in the cause of the Guises, of a dearth of recruits for Scotland, of heretics burnt and heretics rescued, of factions in religion fomented by the great.   Something was very wrong in France, for envoys came thence with soft words.   " Strike now," was Throckmorton's counsel ; " they only seek to gain time."   So a pact was signed at Berwick (February 27, 1560) between Norfolk and the Scottish lords who acted on behalf of " the second person of the realm of Scotland."   Elizabeth   took   Scotland, its   liberties, its   nobility, its expectant heir under her protection, and the French were to be expelled. On second thoughts nothing was published about " the profession of Christ's true religion."   Every French envoy spoke softer than the last. Mary Stewart had assumed the arms of England because she was proud of being Elizabeth's cousin.   The title of Queen of England was taken to annoy, not Elizabeth, but Mary Tudor.   All this meant the Tumult of Amboise (March 14–20).   Behind   that   strange essay in   rebellion, behind la Renaudie, men have seen Condé, and behind Condé two dim figures, Jean Calvin and the English Queen.   Calvin's acquittal seems deserved.   The profession of Christ's true religion was not to be advanced by so ill laid a plot.   But a very ill laid plot might cripple France at this critical moment, and, before we absolve Elizabeth, we wish to know why a certain Tremaine was sent to Britanny, where the plotters were gathering, and whether Chantonnay, Granvelle's brother, was right in saying that la Renaudie had been at the English Court.   Certain it is that Throckmorton had intrigued with Anthony of Navarre, with the Vidame of Chartres, with every enemy of the Guises ; he was an apt pupil in the school that Renard and Noailles had founded in England. A little later (May 23) messages from Condé to the Queen were going round by Strassburg; and in June Tremaine brought from France a scheme which would put Breton or Norman towns into English hands: a scheme from which Cecil as yet recoiled as from " a bottomless pit."

Be all this as it may, the tumult of Amboise fell pat into Cecil's scheme, and on the 29th of March Lord Grey crossed the border with English troops. The Scottish affair then takes this shape:—A small but disciplined force of Frenchmen in the fortified town of Leith; the Regent in Edinburgh Castle, which is held by the neutral Erskine; English ships in the Forth; an English and Scottish army before Leith; very few Scots openly siding with the Queen-mother; the French seeking to gain time. We hasten to the end. An assault failed, but hunger was doing its work. The Regent died on the 11th of June; even stern Protestants have a good word for the gallant woman. Cecil went into Scotland to negotiate with French plenipotentiaries. He wrung from them the Treaty of Edinburgh, which was signed on the 6th of July. The French troops were to quit Scotland. The French King and Queen were never thereafter to use the arms and style of England. Compensation for the insult to her title was to be awarded to Elizabeth by arbitrators or the King of Spain. A pact concluded between Francis and Mary on the one hand and their Scottish subjects on the other was to be observed. That pact itself was humiliating. There was to be pardon for the insurgents; there were to be but six score French soldiers in the land; a Scottish Council was to be appointed:—in a word, Scotland was to be for the Scots. But the lowest point was touched when the observance of this pact between sovereign and rebels was made a term in the treaty between England and France. Cecil and famine were inexorable. We had to sign, said the French commissioners, or four thousand brave men would have perished before our eyes and Scotland would have been utterly lost.

And so the French troops were deported from Scotland and the English army came home from a splendid exploit. The military display, it is true, had not been creditable; there had been disunion, if no worse, among the captains; there had been peculation, desertion, sheer cowardice. All the martial glory goes to the brave besieged. But for the first time an English army marched out of Scotland leaving gratitude behind. Perhaps the truest victory that England had won was won over herself. Not a word had been publicly said of that old suzerainty; no spoil had been taken, not a town detained. Knox included in his liturgy a prayer that there might nevermore be war between Scotland and England, and that prayer has been fulfilled. There have been wars between British factions, but never another truly national war between the two nations. Elizabeth in her first two years " had done what none of her ancestors could do, for by the occasion of her religion she had obtained the amity of Scotland, and thus had God blemished the fame of the great men of the world through the doings of a weak woman":—such was the judgment of a daughter of France and a mother in the Protestant Israel, of Renée, the venerable Duchess of Ferrara. Another observer, Hubert Languet, said that the English were so proud of the conversion of Scotland that they were recovering their old insolence and would be the very people to defy the imminent Council at Trent. The tone of Catholic correspondence changes: the Elizabeth who was merely rushing to her ruin, will now set all Europe alight in her downward course. That young woman's conduct, when we now examine it, will not seem heroic. As was often to happen in coming years, she had been pursuing two policies at once, and she was ready to fall back upon an Austrian marriage if the Scottish revolt miscarried. But this was not what men saw at the time. What was seen was that she and Cecil had played and won a masterly game; and Englishmen must have felt that the change of religion coincided with a transfer of power from incapable to capable hands.

All this had been done, not only without Spanish help, but (so a patriot might say) in defiance of Spain. To discover Philip's intentions had been difficult, and in truth he had been of two minds. Elizabeth was setting the worst of examples. Say what she would, she was encouraging a Protestant revolt against a Catholic King. She was doing this in sight, and with the hardly concealed applause, of the Netherlanders; a friar who dared to preach against her at Antwerp went in fear of his life; whole families of Flemings were already taking refuge in England. Philip's new French wife was coming home to him; his mother-in-law, Catharine de' Medici, implored him to stop Elizabeth from "playing the fool." He had in some kind made himself responsible for the religious affairs of England, by assuring the Pope that all would yet be well. But the intense dread of France, the outcome of long wars, could not be eradicated, and was reasonable enough. He dared not let the French subdue Scotland and threaten England on both sides. Moreover he was for the moment miserably poor; Margaret of Parma, his Regent in the Netherlands, had hardly a crown for current expenses, and the Estates would grant nothing. So in public he scolded and lectured Elizabeth, while in private he hinted that what she was doing should be done quickly. The French, too, though they asked his aid, hardly wished him to fulfil his promise of sending troops to Scotland. Then his navy was defeated by the opportune Turk (May 11); and the Spaniards suspected that the French, if guiltless of, were not displeased at the disaster.

This was not all. The Pope also had been humiliated. The conciliatory Pius IV had not long been on the throne before he sent to Elizabeth a courteous letter (May 5, 1560). Vincent Parpaglia, the Abbot of San Solutore at Turin, once the secretary of Cardinal Pole, was to carry it to her as Nuncio. She was to lend him her ear, and a strong hint was given to her that she could be legitimated. When she heard that the Nuncio was coming, she was perhaps a little frightened; the choice between recantation and the anathema seemed to lie before her; so she talked catholically with the Spanish ambassador. But Philip, when he heard the news, was seriously offended. He saw a French intrigue, and the diplomatic machinery of the Spanish monarchy was set in motion to procure the recall of the Nuncio. All manner of reasons could be given to the Pope to induce a cancellation of his rash act. Pius was convinced or overawed. Margaret of Parma stopped Parpaglia at Brussels. How to extricate the Pope from the adventure without loss of dignity was then the difficult question. Happily it could be said that Pole's secretary was personally distasteful to Philip, who had once imprisoned Parpaglia as a French spy. So at Brussels he enjoyed himself for some months, then announced to Elizabeth that after all he was not coming to her, and in the friendliest way sent her some Italian gossip (September 8). He said that he should go back by Germany, and, when he turned aside to France, Margaret of Parma knew what to think : namely, that there had been a French plot to precipitate a collision between Pius and Elizabeth. At the French Court the disappointed Nuncio "made a very lewd discourse of the Queen, her religion and proceedings." As to Elizabeth, she had answered this first papal approach by throwing the Catholic Bishops into prison. And then, it is to be feared that she, or someone on her behalf, told how the Pope had offered to confirm her Book of Common Prayer, if only she would fall down and worship him.

In August, 1560, a Parliament met at Edinburgh, to do for Scotland what the English Parliament had done in 1559. The Pope's authority was rejected, and the Mass was abolished. Upon a third conviction the sayer or hearer of mass was to be put to death. A Confession of Faith had been rapidly compiled by Knox and his fellow preachers; it is said that Lethington toned down asperities. "To see it pass in such sort as it did" surprised Elizabeth's envoy Randolph. The Scot was not yet a born theologian. Lethington hinted that further amendments could be made if Elizabeth desired them (September 13), and she made bold to tell the Lutheran princes that Scotland had received "the same religion that is used in Almaine"(December 30). The Reforming preachers were few, but the few earnest Catholics were cowed. "This people of a later calling," as an English preacher called the Scots, had not known the disappointment of a young Josiah's reign, and heard the word with gladness. There were wide differences, however, between the proceedings of the two Parliaments. The English problem was comparatively simple. Long before 1559 the English Church had been relieved of superfluous riches; there was only a modest after-math for the Elizabethan scythe. In Scotland the kirk-lands were broad, and were held by prelates or quasi-prelates who were turning Protestant or were closely related to Lords of the Congregation. Catholic or Calvinist, the possessor meant to keep a tight grip on the land. The Bishops could be forbidden to say mass; some of them had no desire to be troubled with that or any other duty; but the decent Anglican process, which substitutes an Edmund Grindal for an Edmund Bonner, could not be imitated. The Scottish lords, had they wished it, could not have thrust an ecclesiastical supremacy upon their Catholic Queen; but to enrich the Crown was not their mind. The new preachers naturally desired something like that proprietary continuity which had been preserved in England: the patrimony of the Church should sustain the new religion. They soon discovered that this was "a devout imagination." They had to construct an ecclesiastical polity on new lines, and they set to work upon a Book of Discipline. Elementary questions touching the relation between Church and State were left open. Even the proceedings of the August Parliament were of doubtful validity. Contrary to wont, a hundred or more of the "minor barons" had formed a part of the assembly. Also, it was by no means clear that the compact signed by the French envoys authorised a Parliament to assemble and do what it pleased in matters of religion.

An excuse had been given to the French for a refusal to ratify the treaty with England. That treaty confirmed a convention which the Scots were already breaking. Another part of the great project was not to be fulfilled. Elizabeth was not going to marry Arran, though the Estates of Scotland begged this of her and set an united kingdom of Great Britain and Ireland before her eyes. Perhaps it was well that Arran was crazy; otherwise there might have been a premature enterprise. A King of Scots who was husband of the English Queen would have been hateful in England; Scotland was not prepared for English methods of government; and Elizabeth had troubles enough to face without barbaric blood feuds and a Book of Discipline. She had gained a great advantage. Sudden as had been the conversion of Scotland, it was permanent. Beneath all that was fortuitous and all that was despicable, there was a moral revolt. "It is almost miraculous," wrote Randolph in the June of 1560, "to see how the word of God takes place in Scotland. They are better willing to receive discipline than in any country I ever was in. Upon Sunday before noon and after there were at the sermons that confessed their offences and repented their lives before the congregation. Cecil and Dr Wotton were present....They think to see next Sunday Lady Stonehouse, by whom the Archbishop of St Andrews has had, without shame, five or six children, openly repent herself." Elizabeth, the deliverer of Scotland, had built an external buttress for her English Church. If now and then Knox "gave her cross and candles a wipe," he none the less prayed for her and everlasting friendship. They did not love each other; but she had saved his Scottish Reformation, and he had saved her Anglican Settlement.

Then, at the end of this full year, there was a sudden change in France. Francis II died (December 5, 1560); Mary was a childless widow;

the Guises were only the uncles of a dowager. A mere boy, Charles IX, was King; power had passed to his mother, Catharine de' Medici and the Bourbons. They had no interest in Mary's claim on England, and, to say the least, were not fanatical Catholics. After some hesitation Mary resolved to return to Scotland. She had hoped for the hand of Philip's son, Don Carlos; but her mother-in-law had foiled her. The kingdom that had been conveyed to the Valois was not to be transferred to the Habsburg, and a niece of the Guises was not to seat herself upon the throne of Spain. The Scottish nobles were not averse to Mary's return, as Elizabeth would not marry Arran and there was thus no longer any fear that Scotland would be merged in France. Mary was profuse of kind words; she won Lord James to her side, and even Lethington was given to understand that he could make his peace. The treaty with England she would not confirm; she would wait until she could consult the Scottish Estates. Elizabeth regarded this as a dangerous insult. Her title to the Crown had been challenged, and the challenge was not withdrawn. Mary's request for a safe-conduct through England was rejected. Orders were given for stopping the ship that bore her towards Scotland, but apparently were cancelled at the last minute. She landed at Leith on the 19th of August, 1561. The long duel between the two Queens began. The story of it must be told elsewhere; but here we may notice that for some years the affairs of Scotland were favourable to the Elizabethan religion. Mary issued a proclamation (August 25, 1561) strikingly similar to that which came from Elizabeth on the first day of her reign. "The state of religion" which Mary "found publicly and universally standing at her home-coming was to be maintained until altered by her and the Estates of the realm." But she and the Estates were not at one, and her religious position was that of a barely tolerated nonconformist. Lord James and Lethington were her chief advisers, and her first military adventure was a successful contest with turbulent but Catholic Gordons. Also it pleased her to hold out hopes that she might accept Elizabeth's religion, if her claim to be Elizabeth's heir presumptive were conceded. The ratification of the treaty she still refused, asserting (a late afterthought) that some words in it might deprive her of her right to succeed Elizabeth if Elizabeth left no issue. She desired to meet Elizabeth; Elizabeth desired to meet her; and the Scottish Catholics said that Mary would not return as "a true Christian woman" from the projected interview. Her uncles were out of power. It was the time of the colloquy of Poissy (September, 1561); it was rumoured that Theodore Beza was converting the Duke of Guise, who talked pleasantly with Throckmorton about the English law of inheritance. The Cardinal of Lorraine publicly flirted with Lutheranism. Elizabeth learnt that her cross and candles marked her off from mere Calvinian Huguenots, though she kept in close touch with Condé and the Admiral. Moreover, the English Catholics were slow to look to

Scotland for a deliverer; the alien's right to inherit was very dubious; they looked rather to young Darnley, who was born in England and by English law was an Englishman and the son of an English mother. So the Elizabethan religion had a fair chance of striking root before the General Council could do its work.

The invitation to the General Council came, and was flatly refused (May 5, 1561). At this point we must turn for one moment to an obscure and romantic episode. From the first days of her reign the English Queen had shown marked favour to her master of the horse, Lord Robert Dudley—a young man, handsome and accomplished, ambitious and unprincipled; the son of that Duke of Northumberland who set Jane Grey on the throne and died as a traitor. Dudley was a married man, but lived apart from his wife, Amy, the daughter of Sir John Robsart. Gossip said that he would kill her and marry the Queen. On the 8th of September, 1560, when he was with the Queen at Windsor, his wife's corpse was found with broken neck at the foot of a staircase in Cumnor Hall. Some people said at once that he had procured her death; and that story was soon being told in all the Courts of Europe; but we have no proof that it was generally believed in England after a coroner's jury had given a verdict which, whatever may have been its terms, exculpated the husband. Dudley (the Leicester of after times) had throughout his life many bitter enemies; but none of them, so far as we know, ever mentioned any evidence of his guilt that a modern English judge would dream of leaving to a jury. We should see merely the unscrupulous character of the husband and the violent, opportune and not easily explicable death of the wife, were it not for a letter that the Spanish ambassador wrote to Margaret of Parma. That letter was not sent until its writer knew of Amy's death (which he mentioned in a postscript), but it professed to tell of what had passed between him, the Queen and Cecil at some earlier, but not precisely defined moment of time. It suggests (as we read it) that Elizabeth knew that Dudley was about to kill his wife. Cecil, it asserts, desired the ambassador to intervene and reduce his mistress to the path of virtue. Those who are inclined to place faith in this wonderful tale about a truly wonderful Cecil, will do well to remember that a postscript is sometimes composed before any part of the letter is written, and that Alvaro de la Quadra, Bishop of Aquila, was suspected by the acute Throckmorton of taking the pay of the Guises. At that moment the rulers of France were refusing ratification of the Edinburgh treaty, and were much concerned that Philip should withdraw his support from Elizabeth. The practical upshot of the letter is that Elizabeth has plunged into an abyss of infamy, will probably be deposed in favour of the Protestant Earl of Huntingdon (Henry Hastings), and will be imprisoned with her favourite. The sagacity of the man who wrote this can hardly be saved, except at the expense of his honesty. Howbeit, Elizabeth, whether she loved Dudley or no (and this will never be known) behaved as if she had thoughts of marrying him, and showed little regard for what was said of his crime. One reading of her character, and perhaps the best, makes her heartless and nearly sexless, but for that reason indecorously desirous of appearing to the world as both the subject and the object of amorous passions. Also she was being pestered to marry the Archduke Charles, who would not come to be looked at, or Arran who had been looked at and rejected. Then (January, 1561) there was an intrigue between the Bishop of Aquila and the suspected murderer. Philip was to favour the Queen's marriage with the self-made widower, and the parties to this unholy union were thenceforth to be good Catholics, or at any rate were to subject themselves and the realm to the authority of the General Council.

There was superabundant falsehood on all sides. Quadra, Dudley, Cecil and Elizabeth, were all of them experts in mendacity, and the exact truth we are not likely to know when they tell the story. But the outcome of it all was that a papal Nuncio, the Abbot Martinengo, coming this time with Philip's full approval, arrived at Brussels with every reason to believe that Elizabeth would favourably listen to the invitation that he was bringing, and then, at the last moment, he learnt that he might not cross the Channel. There are signs that Cecil had difficulty in bringing about this result. Something stood in his way. He had to stimulate the English Bishops into protest, and to discover a little popish plot (there was always one to be discovered) at the right moment. It is conceivable that Dudley and Quadra had for a while ensnared the Queen with hopes of a secure reign and an easy life. It is quite as likely that she was employing them as unconscious agents to keep the Catholics quiet, while important negotiations were pending in France and Germany. That she seriously thought of sending envoys to the Council is by no means improbable; and some stout Protestants held that this was the proper course. But while Quadra and Dudley were concocting their plot, she kept in close alliance with foreign Protestants. Arrangements for a reply to the Pope were discussed with the German Protestant Princes at Naumburg (January, 1561); and strenuous endeavours were made through the puritanic Earl of Bedford to dissuade the French from participation in the Tridentine assembly. The end of it was that the English refusal was especially emphatic, and given in such a manner as to be a rebuff not only to Rome but to Spain. An irritating reference to a recent precedent did not mend matters: King Philip and Queen Mary had repulsed a Nuncio. Another reason could be given. In Ireland the Elizabethan religion, which had been introduced there by Act of Parliament, was not making way. In August, 1560, the Pope, who had already taken upon himself to dispose of two Irish bishoprics, sent to Ireland David Wolfe, a Jesuit priest, and conferred large powers upon him. He seems to have slipped over secretly from Britanny, where he had lain hid. Elizabeth could say, and probably with truth, that his proceedings were hostile to her right and title. As to a Council, of course she was all for a real and true, a "free and general" Council; all Protestants were; but with the papistical affair at Trent she would have nothing to do. Pius had thought better of her; her lover's crypto-Catholicism had been talked of in high places.

The papal Legate at the French Court, the Cardinal of Ferrara, had some hope of succeeding where others had failed: "not as Legate of Rome or the Cardinal of Ferrara, but as Hippolito d'Este," an Italian gentleman devoted to Her Grace's service. There were pleasant letters; cross and candles were commended; she was asked to retain them "even as it were for the Cardinal of Ferrara's pleasure"; but hardly had the Council been re-opened at Trent (January 18, 1562) than Elizabeth was allying herself with the Huguenots and endeavouring to form a Protestant league in Germany. The dream of a France that would peacefully lapse from the Roman obedience was broken at Vassy (March 1, 1562), and the First War of Religion began. In April Sechelles came to England as Condé's envoy and was accredited by Hotman to Cecil. The danger to England was explained by the Queen's Secretary:—The crown of France would be in the hands of the Guisians; the King of Spain would help them; the Queen of Scots would marry Don Carlos; the Council would condemn the Protestants and give their dominions to a Catholic invader (July 20). On the other hand, Calais, Dieppe, or Havre, "perhaps all three," might be Elizabeth's, so some thought; indeed "all Picardy, Normandy, and Gascony might belong to England again." The Queen had been thinking of such possibilities; already in June, 1560, an offer of "certain towns in Britanny and Normandy" had been made to her. She hesitated long, but yielded, and on the 20th of September, 1562, concluded the Treaty of Hampton Court with the Prince of Condé. She was to help with money and men and hold Havre, Dieppe, and Rouen until Calais was restored. It was a questionable step; but Philip was interfering on the Catholic side, and Calais was covetable. Of course she was not at war with Charles IX; far from it; she was bent on delivering the poor lad and his mother from his rebellious subjects, who were also "her inveterate enemies," the Guises. Of religion she said as little as possible; but the Church of which she was the Supreme Governor affirmed in prayer that the Gallican Catholics were enemies of God's Eternal Word, and that the Calvinists were persecuted for the profession of God's Holy Name. The expedition to Havre failed disastrously. After the battle of Dreux (December 19, 1562) and the edict of Amboise (March 19, 1563), all parties in France united to expel the invader. The Earl of Warwick (Ambrose Dudley) and his plague-stricken army were compelled to evacuate Havre after a stubborn resistance (July 28), and the recovery of Calais was further off than ever. Elizabeth had played with the fire once too often. She never after this thought well of Huguenots; and friendship with the ruling powers of France became the central feature of her resolutely pacific policy. However, when at the beginning of 1563 she met her Second Parliament, and the Reformed Church of England held its first Council, all was going well. Since October an English army had once more been holding a French town; a foolhardy plot devised by some young nephews of Cardinal Pole had been opportunely discovered, and the French and Spanish ambassadors were supposed to have had a hand in it. Some notes of Cecil's suggest effective parliamentary rhetoric:

1559 The religion of Christ restored. Foreign authority rejected... 1560 The French at the request of the Scots, partly by force, partly by agreement, sent back to France, and Scotland set free from the servitude of the pope. 1561 The debased copper and brass coinage replaced by gold and silver. England, formerly unarmed, supplied more abundantly than any other country with arms, munitions and artillery. 1562 The tottering Church of Christ in France succoured...

The Queen, it is true, was tormenting her faithful subjects by playing fast and loose with all her many wooers, and by disallowing all talk of what would happen at her death. It was a policy that few women could have maintained, but was sagacious and successful. It made men pray that her days might be long; for, when compared with her sister's, they were good days, and when they were over there would be civil war. We hear the preacher:—" How was this our realm then pestered with strangers, strange gods, strange languages, strange religion, strange coin! And now how peaceably rid of them all!" So there was no difficulty about a supply of money, and another turn might be given to the screw of conformity. Some new classes of persons, members of the House of Commons, lawyers, schoolmasters, were to take the oath of Supremacy; a first refusal was to bring imprisonment and forfeiture, a second death. The temporal lords procured their own exemption on the ground that the Queen was " otherwise sufficiently assured" of their loyalty. That might be so, but she was also sufficiently assured of a majority in the Upper House, for there sat in it four-and-twenty spiritual Lords of her own nomination.

The Spanish ambassador reported (January 14, 1563) that at the opening of this Parliament, the preacher, Nowell, Dean of St Paul's, urged the Queen " to kill the caged wolves," thereby being meant the Marian Bishops. Nowell's sermon is extant, and says too much about the duty of slaying the ungodly. Hitherto the Reformers, the men to whom Cranmer and Ridley were dear friends and honoured masters, had shown an admirable self-restraint. A few savage words had been said, but they had not all come from one side. Christopher Goodman desired that " the bloody Bishops" should be slain; but he had been kept out of England as a dangerous fanatic. Dr John Story, in open Parliament, had gloried in his own cruelty, and had regretted that in Mary's day the axe had not been laid to the root of the tree. At a time when letters from the Netherlands, France or Spain were always telling of burnt Protestants, nobody was burnt in England and very few people lay in prison for conscience sake. The deprived Bishops seem to have been left at large until Parpaglia's mission; then they were sent to gaol. Probably they could be lawfully imprisoned as contumacious excommunicates. Martinengo's advent induced Cecil to clap his hand on a few "mass-mongers," and on some laymen who had held office under Mary. But in these years of horror it is a small matter if a score of Catholics are kept in that Tower where Elizabeth was lately confined; and her preachers had some right to speak of an unexampled clemency.

Rightly or wrongly, but very naturally, there was one man especially odious to the Protestants. When the statute of 1563 was passed, it was said among the Catholics that Bonner would soon be done to death, and the oath that he had already refused was tendered to him a second time by Horne the occupant of the see of Winchester. The tender was only valid if Horne was "Bishop of the diocese." Bonner, who, it is said, had the aid of Plowden, the most famous pleader of the time, threatened to raise the fundamental question whether Horne and his fellows were lawful Bishops. He was prepared to dispute the validity of the statutes of 1559: to dispute the validity of the quasi-papal power of "supplying defects" which the Queen had assumed: to attack the very heart of the new order of things. Elizabeth, however, was not to be hurried into violence. The proceedings against him were stayed; her Bishops were compelled to petition the Parliament of 1566 for a declaration that they were lawful Bishops; their prayer was not granted except with the proviso that none of their past acts touching life and property were to be thereby validated; and eleven out of some thirty-five temporal Lords were for leaving Dr Parker and his suffragans in their uncomfortably dubious position. Elizabeth allowed Lords and Commons to discuss and confirm her letters patent; she was allowing all to see that no Catholic who refrained from plots need fear anything worse than twelve-penny fines; but she had not yet been excommunicated and deposed.

A project for excommunication and deposition was sent to Trent from Louvain, where the Catholic exiles from England congregated. Like Knox and Goodman in Mary's reign, those who had fled from persecution were already setting themselves to exasperate the persecutor. The plan that found favour with them in 1563 involved the action of the Emperor's son, the Archduke Charles. He was to marry Mary Stewart (who, however, had set her heart on a grander match), and then he was to execute the papal ban. Englishmen, it was said, would never again accept as King the heir to the throne of Spain; but his Austrian kinsman would be an unexceptionable candidate or conqueror. The papal Legates at Trent consulted the Emperor, who told his ambassadors that if the Council wished to make itself ridiculous, it had better depose Elizabeth; he and his would have nothing to do with this absurd and dangerous scheme (June 19). Soon afterwards he was allowing his son's marriage, not with the Catholic Mary, but with the heretical Elizabeth, to be once more discussed, and the negotiations for this union were being conducted by the eminently Lutheran Duke of Württemberg, who apparently thought that pure religion would be the gainer if a Habsburg, Ferdinand's son and Maximilian's brother, became King of a Protestant England. Philip too, though he had no wish to quarrel with his uncle, began seriously to think that, in the interest of the Catholic faith and the Catholic King, Mary Stewart was right in preferring the Spanish to the Austrian Charles; and at the same time he was being assured from Rome that it was respect for him which had prevented Pius from bringing Elizabeth's case before the assembled Fathers. She was protected from the anathema, which in 1563 might have been a serious matter, by conflicting policies of the worldliest sort. The only member of the English episcopate who was at Trent, the fugitive Marian Bishop of St Asaph, might do his worst; but the safe course for ecclesiastical power was to make a beginning with Jeanne d'Albret and wait to see whether any good would come of the sentence. Ferdinand, however, begged Elizabeth to take pity on the imprisoned prelates, and she quartered most of them upon their Protestant successors. The English Catholics learnt from the Pope, whom they consulted through the Spanish ambassadors at London and Rome, that they ought not to attend the English churches (October, 1562). As a matter of expediency this was a questionable decision. It is clear that the zealous Romanists over-estimated the number of those Englishmen whose preference for the old creed could be blown into flame. The State religion was beginning to capture the neutral nucleus of the nation, and the irreconcilable Catholics were compelled to appear as a Spanish party secretly corresponding with the Pope through Quadra and Vargas.

Simultaneously with the Parliament a Convocation of the province of Canterbury was held (January 12, 1563), and its acts may be said to complete the great outlines of the Anglican settlement. A delicate task lay before the theologians: no other than that of producing a confession of faith. Happily in this case also a restoration was possible. In the last months of Edward's reign a set of forty-two Articles had been published; in the main they were the work of Cranmer. In 1563 Parker laid a revised version of them before the assembled clergy, and, when a few more changes had been made, they took durable shape and received the royal assent. A little more alteration at a later day made them the famous "Thirty-nine Articles." To all seeming the leaders of English theological thought were remarkably unanimous.

A dangerous point had been passed. Just at the moment when the Roman Church was demonstrating on a grand scale its power of defining dogma, its adversaries were becoming always less hopeful of

Protestant unanimity. In particular, as Elizabeth was often hearing from Germany, the dispute about the Lord's Supper was not to be composed, and a quarrel among divines was rapidly becoming a cause of quarrel among Princes. Well intentioned attempts to construct elastic phrases had done more harm than good, and it was questionable whether the Religious Peace would comprehend the Calvinising Palsgrave. As causes of political union and discord, all other questions of theology were at this moment of comparatively small importance; the line which would divide the major part of the Protestant world into two camps, to be known as Lutheran and Calvinist, was being drawn by theories of the Holy Supper. It is usual and for the great purposes of history it is right to class the Knoxian Church of Scotland as Calvinian, though about Predestination its Confession of Faith is as reticent as are the English Articles. Had it been possible for the English Church to leave untouched the hotly controverted question, the Queen would have been best pleased. She knew that at Hamburg, Westphal, a champion of militant Lutheranism, " never ceased in open pulpit to rail upon England and spared not the chiefest magistrates "; it was he who had denounced the Marian exiles as "the devil's martyrs." Since the first moment of her reign Christopher of Württemberg and Peter Paul Vergerio had been endeavouring to secure her for the Lutheran faith. Jewel, who was to be the Anglican apologist, heard with alarm of the advances made by the ex-Bishop of Capo d' Istria; and the godly Duke had been pained at learning that no less than twenty-seven of the Edwardian Articles swerved from the Augustan standard. Very lately he had urged the Queen to stand fast for a Real Presence. Now, Lutheranism was by this time politically respectable. When there was talk of a Bull against Elizabeth, the Emperor asked how a distinction was to be made between her and the Lutheran Princes, and could take for granted that no Pope with his wits about him would fulminate a sentence against those pillars of the Empire, Augustus of Saxony and Joachim of Brandenburg. When a few years later (1570) a Pope did depose Elizabeth, he was careful to accuse her of participation in " the impious mysteries of Calvin," by which, no doubt, he meant the *Cène.* But though the Augustan might be the safer creed, she would not wish to separate herself from the Huguenots or the Scots, and could have little hope of obtaining from her Bishops a declaration that would satisfy the critical mind of the good Christopher. Concessions were made to him at points where little was at stake; words were taken from his own Württemberg Confession. When the perilous spot was reached, the English divines framed an Article which, as long experience has shown, can be signed by men who hold different opinions; but a charge of deliberate ambiguity could not fairly be brought against the Anglican fathers. In the light of the then current controversy we may indeed see some desire to give no needless offence to Lutherans, and apparently the Queen suppressed until 1571 a phrase which would certainly have repelled them; but, even when this phrase was omitted, Beza would have approved the formula, and it would have given greater satisfaction at Geneva and Heidelberg than at Jena or Tübingen. A papistical controversialist tried to insert a wedge which would separate a Lutheran Parker from an Helvetic Grindal; but we find Parker hoping that Calvin, or, if not Calvin, then Vermigli will lead the Reformers at Poissy, and the only English Bishop to whom Lutheran leanings can be safely attributed held aloof from his colleagues and was for a while excommunicate. It was left for Elizabeth herself to suggest by cross and candles that (as her German correspondents put it) she was living " according to the divine light, that is, the Confession of Augsburg," while someone assured the Queen of Navarre that these obnoxious symbols had been removed from the royal chapel. As to " the sacrifices of masses," there could be no doubt. The anathema of Trent was frankly encountered by " blasphemous fable." Elizabeth knew that her French ambassador remained ostentatiously seated when the Host was elevated, for " reverencing the sacrament was contrary to the usages established by law in England."

Another rock was avoided. Ever since 1532 there had been in the air a project for an authoritative statement of English Canon Law. In Edward's day that project took the shape of a book (*Reformatio Legum Ecclesiasticarum*) of which Cranmer and Peter Martyr were the chief authors, but which had not received the King's sanction when death took him. During Elizabeth's first years we hear of it again; but nothing decisive was done. The draft code that has come down to us has every fault that it could have. In particular, its list of heresies is terribly severe, and apparently (but this has been doubted) the obstinate heretic is to go the way that Cranmer went: not only the Romanists but some at least of the Lutherans might have been relinquished to the secular arm. Howbeit, the scheme fell through. Under a statute of Henry VIII so much of the old Canon Law as was not contrariant nor repugnant to the Word of God or to Acts of the English Parliament was to be administered by the Courts of the English Church. Practically this meant, that the officials of the Bishops had a fairly free hand in declaring law as they went along. They were civilians; the academic study of the Canon Law had been prohibited; they were not in the least likely to contest the right of the temporal legislature to regulate spiritual affairs. And the hands of the Queen's ecclesiastical commissioners were free indeed. Large as were the powers with which she could entrust them by virtue of the Act of Supremacy, she professedly gave them yet larger powers, for they might punish offenders by fine and imprisonment, and this the old Courts of the Church could not do. A constitutional question of the first magnitude was to arise at this point. But during the early years of the reign the commissioners seem to be chiefly employed in depriving papists of their benefices, and this was lawful work.

But while there was an agreeable harmony in dogma and little controversy over polity, the quarrel about ceremonies had begun. In the Convocation of 1563, resolutions, which would have left the posture of the communicants to the discretion of the Bishops and would have abolished the observance of Saints' days, the sign of the cross in baptism and the use of organs, were rejected in the Lower House by the smallest of majorities. It was notorious that some of the Bishops favoured only the simplest rites; five deans and a dozen archdeacons petitioned against the modest surplice. But for its Supreme Governor, the English Church would in all likelihood have carried its own purgation far beyond the degree that had been fixed by the secular legislature. To the Queen, however, it was of the first importance that there should be no more changes before the face of the Tridentine enemy, and also that her occasional professions of Augustan principles should have some visible support. The Bishops, though at first with some reluctance, decided to enforce the existing law; and in course of time conservative sentiment began to collect around the rubrics of the Prayer Book. However, there were some men who were not to be pacified. The "Vestiarian controversy" broke out. Those who strove for a worship purified from all taint of popery (and who therefore were known as "Puritans") "scrupled" the cap and gown that were to be worn by the clergy in daily life, and "scrupled" the surplice that was to be worn in church. Already in 1565 resistance and punishment had begun. At Oxford the Dean of Christ Church was deprived, and young gentlemen at Cambridge discarded the rags of the Roman Antichrist.

In the next year the London clergy were recalcitrant. The Spanish ambassador improved the occasion. In reply, Elizabeth told him that the disobedient ministers were "not natives of the country, but Scotsmen, whom she had ordered to be punished." Literal truth she was not telling, and yet there was truth of a sort in her words. From this time onwards, the historian of the English Church must be often thinking of Scotland, and the historian of the Scottish Church must keep England ever in view. Two kingdoms are drifting together, first towards a "personal" and then towards a "real" Union; but two Churches are drifting apart into dissension and antagonism. The attractions and repulsions that are involved in this process fill a large page in the annals of Britain; they have become plain to all in the age of the Bishops' Wars and the Westminster Assembly; but they are visible much earlier. The attempt to Scoticise the English Church, which failed in 1660, and the attempt to Anglicise the Scottish Church, which failed in 1688, each of these had its century.

For a while there is uncertainty. At one moment Maitland is sure that the two kingdoms have one religion; at another (March, 1563) he can tell the Bishop of Aquila that there are great differences; but undoubtedly in 1560 the prevailing belief was that the Protestants of England and Scotland were substantially at one; and, many as were to be the disputes between them, they remained substantially at one for the greatest of all purposes until there was no fear that either realm would revert to Rome. From the first the Reforming movement in the northern kingdom had been in many ways an English movement. Then in 1560 Reformation and national deliverance had been effected simultaneously by the aid of English gold and English arms. John Knox was a Scot of Scots, and none but a Scot could have done what he did; but, had he died in 1558 at the age of fifty-three, his name would have occurred rather in English than in Scottish books, and he might have disputed with Hooper the honour of being the progenitor of the English Puritans. The congregation at Geneva for which he compiled his Prayer Book was not Scottish but English. His Catholic adversaries in Scotland said that he could not write good Scots. Some of his principal lieutenants were Englishmen or closely connected with England. John Willock, while he was "Superintendent" (Knoxian Bishop) of Glasgow, was also parson of Loughborough. "Mr Goodman of England" had professed divinity at Oxford, and after his career in Scotland was an English archdeacon, though a troublesome Puritan. John Craig had been tutor in an English family, and, instead of talking honest Scots, would "knap suddrone." But further, Knox had signed the English Articles of 1553, and is plausibly supposed to have modified their wording. A Catholic controversialist of Mary's day said that "a runagate Scot" had procured that the adoration of Christ in the Sacrament should be put out of the English Prayer Book. To that book in 1559 Knox had strong objections; he detested ceremonies; the Coxian party at Frankfort had played him a sorry trick and he had just cause of resentment; but there was nothing doctrinally wrong with the Book. It was used in Scotland. In 1560 a Frenchman whom Randolph took to church in Glasgow, and who had previously been in Elizabeth's chapel, saw great differences, but heard few, for the prayers of the English Book were said. Not until some years later did "the Book of Geneva" (Knox's liturgy) become the fixed standard of worship for the Scottish Church. The objection to all prescript prayers is of later date and some say that it passes from England into Scotland. This Genevan Use had been adopted by the chaplain of Elizabeth's forces at Havre, and, though he was bidden to discontinue it, he was forthwith appointed to the deanery of Durham. A Puritan movement in England there was likely to be in any case. The arguments of both parties were already prepared. The Leipzig *Interim*, the work of the Elector Maurice, had given rise to a similar quarrel among the Lutherans, between Flacians on the one side and Philipians on the other, over those rites and ornaments which were "indifferent" in themselves, but had, as some thought, been soiled by superstition. The English exiles who returned from Zurich and Geneva would dislike cap, gown, and surplice; but their foreign mentors counselled submission ; Bullinger was large-minded, and Calvin was politic. Scotland, however, was very near, and in Scotland this first phase of Puritanism was in its proper place. So long as Mary reigned there and plotted there, the Protestant was hardly an established religion ; and, had Knox been the coolest of schemers, he would have endeavoured to emphasise every difference between the old worship and the new. It was not for him to make light of *adiaphora* ; it was for him to keep Protestant ardour at fever heat. Maitland, who was a cool schemer, made apology to Cecil for Knox's vehemence : " as things are fallen out, it will serve to good purpose." And yet it is fairly certain that Knox dissuaded English Puritans from secession. In his eyes the Coxian Church of England might be an erring sister, but still was a twin sister, of the Knoxian Church of Scotland.

Elizabeth's resistance to the Puritan demands was politic. The more Protestant a man was, the more secure would be his loyalty if Rome were aggressive. It was for her to appeal to the " neutral in religion " and those " faint professors " of whom her Bishops saw too many. It is not perhaps very likely that surplices and square caps won to her side many of those who cared much for the old creed. Not the simplest and most ignorant papist, says Whitgift to the Puritans, could mistake the Communion for the Mass : the Mass has been banished from England as from Scotland . we are full as well Reformed as are the Scots. But Elizabeth feared frequent changes, was glad to appear as a merely moderate Reformer, and meant to keep the clergy well in hand. Moreover, in Catholic circles her cross and candles produced a good impression. When she reproved Dean Nowell for inveighing against such things, this was soon known to Cardinal Borromeo, and he was not despondent (April 21, 1565). Even her dislike for a married clergy, which seems to have been the outcome of an indiscriminating misogyny, was favourably noticed. It encouraged the hope that she might repent, and for some time Rome was unwilling to quench this plausibly smoking flax. But her part was difficult. The Puritans could complain that they were worse treated than Spanish, French and Dutch refugees, whose presence in England she liberally encouraged. Casiodoro de Reyna, Nicolas des Gallars, and Utenhove, though the Bishop of London was their legal " superintendent," were allowed a liberty that was denied to Humphry and Sampson ; there was one welcome for Mrs Matthew Parker and another for Madame la Cardinale.

The controversy of the sixties over rites and clothes led to the controversy of the seventies over polity, until at length Presbyterianism and Episcopalianism stood arrayed against each other. But the process was gradual. We must not think that Calvin had formulated a Presbyterian system, which could be imported ready-made from Geneva to

Britain. In what is popularly called Presbyterianism there are various elements. One is the existence of certain presbyters or elders, who are not pastors or ministers of the Word, but who take a larger or smaller part in the government of the Church. This element may properly be called Calvinian, though the idea of some such eldership had occurred to other Reformers. Speculations touching the earliest history of the Christian Church were combined with a desire to interest the laity in a rigorous ecclesiastical discipline. But Calvin worked with the materials that were ready to his hand and was far too wary to raise polity to the rank of dogma. The Genevan Church was essentially civic or municipal; its Consistory is very much like a committee of a town council. This could not be the model for a Church of France or of Scotland, which would contain many particular congregations or churches. Granted that these particular Churches will be governed by elders, very little has yet been decided: we may have the loosest federation of autonomous units, or the strictest subordination of the parts to some assembly which is or represents the whole. Slowly and empirically, the problem was solved with somewhat different results in France, Scotland, and the Low Countries. As we have said, the month which saw Knox land in Scotland saw a French Church taking shape in a national Synod that was being secretly held at Paris. Already Frenchmen are setting an example for constituent assemblies and written constitutions. Knox, who had been edifying the Church of Dieppe—that Dieppe which was soon to pass into Elizabeth's hands—stood in the full current of the French movement; but, like his teacher, he had no iron system to impose. Each particular congregation would have elders besides a pastor; there would be some general assembly of the whole Church; but Knox was not an ecclesiastical jurist. The *First Book of Discipline* (1560) decides wonderfully little; even the structure of the General Assembly is nebulous; and, as a matter of fact, all righteous noblemen seem to be welcome therein. It gradually gives itself a constitution, and, while a similar process is at work in France, other jurisdictional and governmental organs are developed, until kirk-session, presbytery, synod and assembly form a concentric system of Courts and councils of which Rome herself might be proud. But much of this belongs to a later time; in Scotland it is not Knoxian but Melvillian.

A mere demand for some ruling elders for the particular Churches was not likely to excite enthusiasm or antagonism. England knew that plan. The curious Church of foreign refugees, which was organised in the London of Edward VI's days under the presidency of John Laski, had elders. Cranmer took great interest in what he probably regarded as a fruitful experiment, and the Knoxian Church has some traits which, so good critics think, tell less of Geneva than of the Polish but cosmopolitan nobleman. Dr Horne, Elizabeth's Bishop of Winchester, had been the pastor of a Presbyterian flock of English refugees at Frankfort. With a portion of that flock he had quarrelled, not for being Presbyterian, but because the Presbyterianism of this precocious conventicle was already taking that acutely democratic and distinctly uncalvinian form, in which the elders are the annually elected officers of a congregation which keeps both minister and elders well under control. Among Englishmen a drift towards Congregationalism appears almost as soon as the ruling elder.

The enthusiasm and antagonism were awakened by a different cry: it was not a call for presbyters, but a call for " parity," for an equality among all the ministers of God's Word, and consequently for an abolition of all " prelacy." As a battle cry this is hardly Calvinian; nor is it Knoxian; it is first audible at Cambridge. The premisses, it is true, lay ready to the hand of anyone who chose to combine them. The major was that Protestant principle which refers us to the primitive Church. The minor was a proposition familiar to the Middle Age:—originally there was no difference between the *presbyter* and the *episcopus*. Every student of the Canon Law knew the doctrine that the prelacy of Bishops is founded, not on divine command, but on a " custom of the Church." When the Puritan said that the episcopal jurisdiction was of popish origin, he agreed with Laynez and the Pope; at least, as had been amply shown at Trent, the divine right of Bishops was a matter over which Catholic doctors could quarrel bitterly. But the great Reformers had been chary of their words about ecclesiastical polity; there were many possibilities to be considered, and the decision would rest with Princes or civic Councils. The defenders of Anglican episcopacy occasionally told the Puritan that he was not a good Calvinist, and even Beza could hardly be brought by British pressure to a sufficiently dogmatic denunciation of prelacy. As to Knox, it is clear that, though he thought the English dioceses too large, he had no radical objection to such prelacy as existed in England. Moreover, the Church that he organised in Scotland was prelatic, and there is but little proof that he regarded its prelatic constitution as a concession to merely temporary needs. The word " bishop " was avoided (in Scotland there still were lawful Bishops of another creed); but over the "dioceses" stand "superintendents" (the title comes from Germany), who, though strictly accountable to the general assembly, are distinctly the rulers of the diocesan clergy. Between superintendent and minister there is no " parity "; the one may command, the other must obey. The theory that valid orders can be conferred by none but a Bishop, Knox would, no doubt, have denied; but some at all events of the contemporary English Bishops would have joined him in the denial.

Apparently Thomas Cartwright, a young professor of divinity at Cambridge, spoke the word (1570) that had not yet been spoken in Scotland. Cambridge was seething with Puritanism; the Bishops had been putting the vestiarian law in force ; and the French Church had declared for parity. "There ought to be an equality": presbyter and Bishop were once all one. But if the demand for parity was first heard south of the Tweed, it was soon echoed back by Scotland; and thenceforth the English Puritan was often looking northward. In Scotland much had been left unsettled. From August, 1561, to May, 1568, Mary Stewart is there; Rizzio and Darnley, Bothwell and Moray, Lethington and Knox, are on the stage; and we hold our breath while the tragedy is played. We forget the background of unsolved questions and uncertain law. Is the one lawful religion the Catholic or the Protestant? Are there two established Churches, or is one Church established and another endowed? There is an *interim*: or rather, an armed truce. The Queen had not confirmed the statutes of 1560, though mass-mongers were occasionally imprisoned. Nothing decisive had been done in the matter of tithes and kirk-lands and advowsons. The Protestant ministers and super-intendents were receiving small stipends which were charged upon the ecclesiastical revenues; but the Bishops and Abbots, some of whom were Protestant ministers, had not been ousted from their temporalities or their seats in Parliament, and, as vacancies occurred, the bishoprics were con-ferred upon new occupants, some of whom were Catholics. The General Assembly might meet twice a year; but John Hamilton still went to Parliament as a reverend father in God and primate of Scotland. If Mary had succeeded in reestablishing Catholicism, we should probably have said that it had never been disestablished. And when she had been deposed and a Parliament held in her son's name had acknowledged the Knoxian Church to be "the immaculate spouse of Christ," much was still unsettled. What was to be done with the bishoprics and abbacies and with the revenues and seats in Parliament that were involved there-with? Grave questions of civil and ecclesiastical polity were open, and a large mass of wealth went a-begging or illustrated the beatitude of possession. Then in the seventies we on the one hand see an attempt to Anglicise the Church by giving it Bishops, who will sit in Parliament and be somewhat more prelatic than were Knox's superintendents, and on the other hand we hear a swelling cry for parity.

To many a Scot prelacy will always suggest another word of evil sound: to wit, Erastianism. The link is Anglican. The name of the professor of medicine at Heidelberg—it was Thomas Liebler, or in Greek Erastus—won a fame or infamy in Britain that has been denied to it elsewhere. And in some sort this is fair, for it was an English Puritan who called him into the field; and after his death his manuscript book was brought to England and there for the first time printed. His Prince, the Elector Palatine Frederick III, was introducing into his dominions, in the place of the Lutheranism which had prevailed there, the theology that flowed from Zurich and Geneva; images were being destroyed and altars were giving place to tables. This, as Elizabeth knew when the Thirty Nine Articles lay before her, was a very serious change; it strained to breaking-point the professed unanimity of the Protestant Princes. Theology, however, was one thing, Church-polity another; and for all the Genevan rigours Frederick was not yet prepared. But to Heidelberg for a doctor's degree came an English Puritan, George Withers, and he stirred up strife there by urging the necessity of a discipline exercised by pastor and elders (June, 1568). Erastus answered him by declaring that excommunication has no warrant in the Word of God; and further that, when the Prince is a Christian, there is no need for a corrective jurisdiction which is not that of the State, but that of the Church. This sowed dissension between Zurich and Geneva: between Bullinger, the friend of the English Bishops, and Beza, the oracle of the Puritans. Controversy in England began to nibble at the Royal Supremacy; and in Scotland the relation between the State (which until 1567 had a papistical head) and the Knoxian Church, was of necessity highly indeterminate. Knox had written sentences which, in our rough British use of the term, were Erastian enough; and a great deal of history might have been changed, had he found in Scotland a pious prince or even a pious princess, a Josiah or even a Deborah. As it fell out, the Scottish Church aspired to, and at times attained, a truly medieval independence. Andrew Melvill's strain of language has been compared with that of Gregory VII; so has Thomas Cartwright's; but the Scottish Church had an opportunity of resuming ancient claims which was denied to the English. In 1572 an oath was imposed in Scotland; the model was English; but important words were changed. The King of Scots is "Supreme Governor of this realm as well in things temporal as in the conservation and purgation of religion." The Queen of England is "Supreme Governor of this realm as well in all spiritual or ecclesiastical things or causes as temporal." The greater continuity of ecclesiastical history is not wholly on one side of the border. The charge of popery was soon retorted against the Puritans by the Elizabethan divines and their Helvetian advisers:— Your new presbyter in his lust for an usurped dominion is but too like old priest.

In controversy with the Puritans the Elizabethan religion gradually assumed an air of moderation which had hardly belonged to it from the first; it looked like a compromise between an old faith and a new. It is true that from the beginning of her reign Elizabeth distrusted Calvin; and when she swore that she never read his books she may have sworn the truth. That blast of the trumpet had repelled her. Not only had "the regiment of women" been attacked, but Knox and Goodman had advocated a divine right of rebellion against idolatrous Princes. Calvin might protest his innocence; but still this dangerous stuff came from his Geneva. Afterwards, however, he took an opportunity of being serviceable to the Queen in the matter of a book which spoke ill of her father and mother. Then a pretty message went to him and he was bidden to feel assured of her favour (September 18, 1561).   Moreover, in German history Elizabeth appears as espousing the cause of oppressed Calvinists against the oppressing Lutherans.   Still as time went on, when the Huguenots, as she said, had broken faith with her about Havre and Calais, and the attack on "her officers," the Bishops, was being made in the name of the Genevan discipline, her dislike of Geneva, its works, and its ways, steadily grew.   Though in the region of pure theology Calvin's influence increased apace in England and Scotland after his death, and Whitgift, the stern repressor of the Puritans, was a remorseless predestinarian, still the Bishops saw, albeit with regret, that they had two frontiers to defend, and that they could not devote all their energy to the confutation of the Louvainists.

Then some severed, or half-severed, bonds were spliced.   Parker was a lover of history, and it was pleasant to sit in the chair of Augustine, seeing to editions of Ælfric's Homilies and the Chronicles of Matthew Paris.   But the work was slowly done, and foreigners took a good share in it.   Hadrian Saravia, who defended English episcopacy against Beza, was a refugee, half Spaniard, half Fleming.   Pierre Baron of Cambridge, who headed a movement against Calvin's doctrine of the divine decrees, was another Frenchman, another pupil of the law-school of Bourges. And it is to be remembered that at Elizabeth's accession the Genevan was not the only model for a radically Reformed Church.   The fame of Zwingli's Zurich had hardly yet been eclipsed, and for many years the relation between the Anglican and Tigurine Churches was close and cordial.   A better example of a purely spiritual power could hardly be found than the influence that was exercised in England by Zwingli's successor Henry Bullinger.   Bishops and Puritans argue their causes before him as if he were the judge.   So late as 1586 English clergymen are required to peruse his immortal *Decades.*   There was some gratitude in the case.   A silver cup with verses on it had spoken Elizabeth's thanks for the hospitality that he had shown to Englishmen.   But that was not all; he sympathised with Elizabeth and her Bishops and her Erastianism.   He condemned "the English fool" who broke the peace of the Palatinate by a demand for the Genevan discipline.   When the cry was that the congregation should elect its minister, the Puritan could be told how in an admirably reformed republic Protestant pastors were still chosen by patrons who might be papists, even by a Bishop of Constance who might be the Pope's own nephew and a Cardinal to boot, for a Christian magistracy would see that this patronage was not abused. And then when the bad day came and the Pope hurled his thunderbolt, it was to Bullinger that the English Bishops looked for a learned defence of their Queen and their creed.   Modestly, but willingly, he undertook the task: none the less willingly perhaps, because Pius V had seen fit to couple Elizabeth's name with Calvin's, and this was a controversialist's trick which Zurich could expose.   Bullinger knew all the

Puritan woes and did not like surplices; he knew and much disliked the "semi-popery" of Lutheran Germany; but in his eyes the Church of England was no half-way house. As to Elizabeth, he saw her as no luke-warm friend of true religion, but as a virgin-queen beloved of God, whose wisdom and clemency, whose felicity and dexterity were a marvel and a model for all Christian Princes (March 12, 1572).

The felicity and dexterity are not to be denied. The Elizabethan religion which satisfied Bullinger was satisfying many other people also; for (to say nothing of intrinsic merits or defects) it appeared as part and parcel of a general amelioration. It was allied with honest money, cheap and capable government, national independence, and a reviving national pride. The long Terror was overpast, at least for a while; the flow of noble blood was stayed; the axe rusted at the Tower. The long Elizabethan peace was beginning (1563), while France was ravaged by civil war, and while more than half the Scots looked to the English Queen as the defender of their faith. One Spaniard complains that these heretics have not their due share of troubles (November, 1562); another, that they are waxing fat upon the spoil of the Indies (August, 1565). The England into which Francis Bacon was born in 1561 and William Shakespeare in 1564 was already unlike the England that was ruled by the Queen of Spain.

Made in the USA
Columbia, SC
17 December 2021

51908472R00030